Why They Hate Us

Selena Arnold

Published by Selena L. L. Arnold, 2024.

This is a fiction work. Names, characters, places, and incidents either are products of the author's imagination or are used fictitiously. Any resemblance to actual events, locales, or persons, living or dead, is entirely coincidental.

First Edition: 2024

ISBN: [ISBN Number, if applicable]

Published by Selena L. L. Arnold

Printed in [United State of America]

Introduction:

Hatred is never simple. It doesn't rise overnight, nor does it dissipate quickly. It is the culmination of fear, misunderstanding, ignorance, and the reluctance to confront uncomfortable truths. This story is an exploration of that hatred—its roots, its consequences, and, ultimately, the possibilities for overcoming it.

In a world where people are increasingly divided, the question of *why* hatred persists looms large. What fuels the distrust and animosity between groups? Why does the cycle of oppression, resentment, and exclusion continue despite progress? These questions are not merely academic. They are lived in realities for millions, carried in the hearts and minds of those who feel the weight of prejudice daily.

"Why They Hate Us" delves into the personal and the political, the internal and the external forces that drive a society to fracture. Through the protagonist's journey, readers will confront the uncomfortable reality of systemic hatred and its corrosive effect on both the oppressed and the oppressors.

This novel is divided into five parts, each representing a phase of this journey: from the early seeds of division to the rising storm of conflict, the war of ideals, and finally, the slow process of rebuilding. Each chapter uncovers a new layer of the story, revealing the complexity of human emotion and societal conflict.

The protagonist's experiences mirror those of so many who have been marginalized, vilified, and demonized. But this is not just a story of suffering. It is a story of resilience, courage, and the unrelenting pursuit of justice. It is about standing up, speaking out, and demanding change in the face of overwhelming odds.

At its heart, "Why They Hate Us" is a story of transformation. It is about the evolution from anger to understanding, from conflict to peace. It asks the reader to reflect on their own biases and prejudices, and to consider what role they play in either perpetuating or dismantling systems of hate.

This novel does not offer easy answers, nor does it shy away from the brutal realities of division. But it does offer hope that by confronting hatred head-on, we can begin to heal the wounds that have divided us for so long.

Chapter 1: The Unspoken Divide

There are some things that are never said aloud, but everyone knows. Like the way the air in a room shifts when certain people enter, or how conversations die down when they walk past. It's subtle, almost imperceptible. But it's there. The looks, the quick glances exchanged between those who feel they belong and those who know they don't.

Aisha had grown up with that feeling, a constant hum in the background of her life. She didn't need to be told she was different, everything around her made it clear. The small town she grew up in, where everyone knew each other's business, had its rules. Some were spoken, but most were understood without needing to be said. And that was where the danger lay.

It was the unspoken divide that hurt the most, the one that wasn't written into laws or posted on signs but was etched into the very fabric of the community. Aisha felt it every day: at school, at the grocery store, at church. She felt it in the way the mothers at the park would glance at her mother before turning back to their children, pretending not to see them. Or the way her teachers would avoid calling on her in class, as if her voice was something to be feared, something to be silenced.

Her mother had always told her to keep her head down, to stay out of trouble. "Don't give them a reason," she'd say. "Don't stand out." But how could she not stand out when everything about her made people uncomfortable? Her skin, her hair, her voice all marked her as different. And in a town like theirs, different was dangerous.

It wasn't just a race. It wasn't just class. It was the way the town had been built, the way the people had been taught to see themselves and others. There were rules—unwritten, unspoken, but always enforced. People like Aisha and her family were meant to know their place, to stay on their side of the invisible line that divided the town into two.

But Aisha had never been good at following rules. Not the ones that told her who she could be friends with or where she could sit in the lunchroom. And certainly not the ones that told her to stay quiet, to be grateful for whatever scraps of acceptance she was offered. She was tired, tired of pretending that the hatred wasn't there, tired of smiling politely while people looked through her as if she didn't exist.

The older she got, the more she realized that the hatred wasn't just directed at her. It was everywhere. It was in the way people talked about the neighboring town, the way they whispered about outsiders as if they were something to be feared. It was in the way the police patrolled certain neighborhoods but not others, the way the local politicians made decisions that seemed designed to keep people like her family in their place.

Hatred was woven into the fabric of the town, as natural as the changing of the seasons. And yet, no one ever talked about it. No one admitted that it was there, festering just beneath the surface. They called it tradition, called it pride. But Aisha knew what it really was. It was fear of change, fear of difference, fear of losing control.

For years, she had tried to keep her head down, to follow her mother's advice. But now, as she stood at the edge of adulthood, Aisha knew that staying silent was no longer an option. The hatred that surrounded her wasn't going to disappear on its own. It was going to take someone to confront it, to call it out for what it was. And Aisha was ready.

The first time she spoke up, it was almost accidental. A heated exchange at a school board meeting about the district's budget cuts—cuts that, unsurprisingly, affected her neighborhood the most. She hadn't planned on saying anything, but as she listened to the dismissive comments, to the way her community was brushed aside as if their children's futures didn't matter, something inside her snapped.

"I'm tired of hearing about how we should be grateful for what we have," she said, her voice trembling but steady. "We deserve better. Our kids deserve better."

The room had gone silent, all eyes on her. For a moment, Aisha thought she had made a mistake, that she had crossed the line her mother had always warned her about. But then, something unexpected happened. People started to nod. A few murmurs of agreement rippled through the crowd. And at that moment, Aisha realized that she wasn't alone.

That was the first time she had stood up and spoken out against the hatred that had always surrounded her. It wouldn't be the last.

Chapter 2: Inherited Hatred

Aisha had always known there was something different about her family. It wasn't just the color of their skin or the neighborhood they lived in, it was deeper than that. The hate directed toward them didn't start with her generation. It was an inheritance, passed down like a burden, as though the very blood in their veins had somehow marked them for disdain.

Her grandmother, Mama Ruth, used to tell stories of how things were "back in the day." She'd sit on the porch, the thin summer breeze stirring the scent of jasmine, and speak in a voice weathered by years of witnessing hardship. The tales she told were never about grand adventures or light-hearted memories. They were heavy, thick with the weight of survival.

"They haven't never liked us," Mama Ruth would say, her voice cracking with age. "Not then, not now. And they'll find any excuse to keep us down."

As a child, Aisha didn't fully understand what her grandmother meant. To her, the stories sounded like something from a different world, a different time—far removed from her own life. But as she grew older, Aisha began to see the patterns. The same hatred that had kept Mama Ruth from certain jobs, from entering certain schools, from walking freely down certain streets, was still alive and well. It had just taken on new shapes, new faces.

Her father, a man of few words, rarely spoke about the past. He carried his history silently, letting his actions and his stoic demeanor do the talking. He had learned to navigate the system in his own way, careful not to provoke, careful to play the part that was expected of him. He was a man who believed in hard work and keeping his head down—much like Aisha's mother. But Aisha had seen the flickers of frustration in his eyes, the moments when he clenched his jaw just a little too tight, or when his hands shook with the effort to hold back his true feelings.

Her father had always warned her about the dangers of pushing too hard, of trying to change things that couldn't be changed. "They don't want us to rise," he'd say. "But you got to be smarter than them. Don't give them any reason to take what little we got."

It was a lesson learned through generations of trial and error. Her family knew, better than most, the consequences of stepping out of line. The hate they faced wasn't just personal; it was institutional. It was written into laws, the economy, and the education system. It was in the way the bank denied her parents a loan when they tried to move to a better neighborhood. It was in the way her school was underfunded, the classrooms overcrowded, and the teachers overstretched.

Yet, despite her parents' warnings, Aisha couldn't shake the feeling that staying quiet, keeping her head down, was just another way of giving in to the hatred that surrounded them. She had heard the stories of generations past, of the fights her ancestors had fought to claim even the smallest bit of freedom, the smallest bit of respect. If they had stayed silent, nothing would have changed. And Aisha wasn't willing to wait for another generation for change to come.

Her parents' generation had learned to survive in the cracks of a broken system. But Aisha wasn't interested in just surviving—she wanted to thrive. And that meant doing something, her family had always warned her against standing up and making her voice heard.

The more Aisha learned about her family's past, the clearer the patterns became. The hatred they faced wasn't random. It was cultivated, carefully maintained through centuries of laws, social norms, and unspoken rules designed to keep people like her in their place. It was built on fear, the fear of losing control, the fear of the unknown, the fear of change. And that fear had been passed down, just as much as the hate.

She often wondered if those on the other side of the divide even realized how deep the hatred ran. Did they know, or were they simply repeating the lessons they had been taught? Aisha couldn't help but think about the kids at school who sneered at her when she walked by, or the mothers who pulled their children close whenever she came near. Had they been born with that hate, or had they learned it, just like her?

Mama Ruth had always said that hate was taught, not inherited. But sometimes it felt like it was poison passed down through generations, seeping into the blood until it became a part of who you were. Aisha didn't want to believe that people were born to hate, but she had seen too many children grow up to become just like their parents—filled with the same venom, the same small-mindedness.

It was a cycle that seemed impossible to break. But Aisha wasn't ready to give up on the idea that things could change. She knew it wouldn't be easy—her grandmother's stories had made that clear enough—but the alternative was unbearable. To live in a world where hate was ruled, where people were kept in their place by invisible chains, was a fate Aisha refused to accept.

Her first act of defiance at the school board meeting had been small—a ripple in an ocean of apathy—but it had stirred something inside her. The people in that room had listened. They had nodded in agreement. And for the first time, Aisha had felt the power of her own voice. It wasn't enough to tear down the walls that divided them, but it was a start.

The next step would be harder. Speaking out was one thing, but challenging the deeply ingrained systems that kept her and her family in their place was something else entirely. It would mean stepping into a role she had never imagined for herself—a leader, an activist, someone who refused to be silenced.

But Aisha knew that if she didn't fight, the cycle of inherited hate would continue. And she couldn't live with that. She couldn't live in a world where her children, and their children, would grow up facing the same hatred that had marked her life, her parents' lives, and the lives of those who came before her.

It was time to break the cycle. Time to stand up, even if it meant standing alone.

Chapter 3: The Family's Legacy

The old family photo albums were tucked away in a wooden chest at the foot of Aisha's bed, gathering dust. She had seen them before, but it wasn't until recently that she had begun to see them differently. When she was a child, those pictures were just fragments of a time long gone, faces she could hardly recognize, stories she barely understood. Now, as she shifted through the pages, each photo seemed to carry the weight of her family's history of struggle, resilience, and survival.

There was a picture of her grandmother, Mama Ruth, in front of a small wooden shack, dressed in her Sunday best. Aisha had always marveled at how proud and dignified her grandmother looked in that photo, even though the world around her had tried so hard to deny her dignity. Mama Ruth had been a fighter, though she rarely spoke of the battles she had faced. It was in her eyes, though, that quiet fire that refused to be extinguished.

Mama Ruth had grown up in the South, in a time when segregation wasn't just a fact of life, but a law. She had lived through the indignities of Jim Crow, the threats of violence for simply existing in a space where she wasn't "supposed" to be. Aisha remembered the stories her grandmother had told stories of walking miles to school because the bus was reserved for white children, of being spat at when she dared to sit at the front of the train, of watching her father get turned away from the voting booth despite his desperate plea to exercise his basic rights.

But Mama Ruth had never bowed to the pressure to disappear, to become invisible. She had raised her children with pride, instilling in them a sense of self-worth that no one could take away. She had been active in her church, one of the few places where black women could find some measure of leadership and respect. She had spoken up when others stayed silent, even when it cost her dearly.

The legacy of resistance didn't start with Mama Ruth, though. Aisha's great-grandfather, Elijah, had been a sharecropper who worked the same land his ancestors had been enslaved on. His life was one of grueling labor, under the thumb of landowners who exploited his hard work, giving him barely enough to feed his family. But Elijah was not a man who accepted his fate quietly.

Though he had little formal education, he knew enough to understand that the system was rigged against him. He had once been jailed for organizing a strike among the sharecroppers, demanding fair wages and decent living conditions. The strike had been broken, of course, and Elijah had spent weeks in a cell, but the seed of defiance had been planted in the family's bloodline.

It was that spirit of defiance, passed down through generations, that had shaped Aisha's father, though he rarely spoke of it. Her father, James, was a man of few words but many burdens. He had been a factory worker for most of his life, working double shifts to put food on the table and keep the roof over their heads. He had seen firsthand how the system worked to keep people like him at the bottom—stuck in jobs that paid just enough to survive but never enough to get ahead.

James had once dreamed of becoming an engineer. He had excelled in math and science in school, and his teachers had encouraged him to pursue a degree. But life had gotten in the way. A job at the factory had come first, then marriage, then children. His dreams had been put on hold, and eventually, they had faded into the background, replaced by the day-to-day grind of survival. Still, he had never lost his sense of justice. He had raised Aisha to see the world for what it was, not through rose-colored glasses, but with a clear understanding of the inequities that surrounded them.

Aisha had always admired her father's quiet strength, but she couldn't help but wonder if there was more, he could have done. If he had pushed harder, if he had fought like her great-grandfather or her grandmother, could their lives have been different? Could they have broken free from the cycle of poverty and struggle that seemed to define their family's legacy?

These questions weighed on her now more than ever. As she flipped through the pages of the photo album, Aisha saw more than just the faces of her ancestors—she saw the fight they had carried with them, a fight that had never really ended. Each generation had pushed a little harder, chipped away at the walls that held them back, but the walls were still there. And now it was her turn.

The photo album was filled with stories of pain, but also of pride. There was her uncle Darrell, who had marched with Dr. King in Selma. There was her aunt Margaret, who had started the first black-owned bookstore in their town. There were cousins and distant relatives who had joined protests, written letters to congressmen, organized voter registration drives. The family was a tapestry of small but significant acts of resistance, woven together by a shared belief that things could be different—better.

But for all their efforts, for all the progress that had been made, Aisha couldn't shake the feeling that too much had stayed the same. The hatred her family had fought against was still there, lurking beneath the surface, sometimes overt, sometimes subtle, but always present. It wasn't just about individual acts of racism or prejudice; it was about a system that had been built to keep people like her family at the margins.

As she looked at the photo of Mama Ruth standing proudly in front of that old shack, Aisha felt a swell of determination rise in her chest. She wasn't going to let her family's legacy end with her. She wasn't going to let the sacrifices of those who came before her be in vain. It was time to take the next step. It was time to do more than just survive.

The school board meeting had just the beginning. There were bigger battles to be fought, systems to dismantle, walls to tear down. Aisha didn't know exactly how she was going to do it, but she knew that she had to try. For her family. For herself. For the generations that would come after her.

The legacy of hate was strong, but Aisha was determined that her family's legacy of resistance would be stronger. And she was ready to fight for it.

worldview and her desire to fight back against the injustices she has witnessed.

Chapter 4: Lessons from Childhood

The first lesson Aisha learned about her place in the world came long before she had the words to describe it. She must have been five or six years old, sitting in the back seat of her father's old sedan as they drove through the nicer part of town. Her father's hands gripped the steering wheel tightly as they passed the wide, tree-lined streets, the perfectly manicured lawns, and the houses that looked like something out of a television show.

"Why don't we live here?" Aisha had asked, her voice filled with innocent curiosity.

Her father hadn't answered right away. He had glanced at her in the rearview mirror, his eyes heavy with something she couldn't understand yet.

"We don't belong here," he had said quietly, the words slipping out as if they carried more weight than he could bear to explain.

At the time, Aisha didn't know what that meant. She had just wanted to live somewhere where the streets weren't cracked, where the houses weren't packed so tightly together, where the air didn't smell like diesel and sweat. She had wanted to live in a place where everything looked perfect, like it did in the neighborhoods they drove past.

It wasn't until later, when she grew older, that she began to understand what her father had really meant. It wasn't just that they didn't have the money to live in those nice houses. It was that people like them—black, working-class, outsiders in a town that prided itself on its "heritage"—weren't welcome there. The boundaries weren't drawn on a map, but they were there all the same, invisible but rigid, like a fence that kept her family out of places they weren't supposed to be.

That was her first lesson about the unspoken rules that governed her world. It wouldn't be her last.

As Aisha grew older, the lines became clearer. There were the obvious signs—like the time her mother had taken her to a local diner, only for them to be ignored by the waitress for so long that they eventually left. But there were more subtle lessons, too, the way certain doors always seemed to be closed to her, even when she followed the rules, worked hard, and did everything she was supposed to do.

At school, it was no different. Aisha had always been a good student, one of the best in her class. But no matter how hard she worked; it seemed like her accomplishments were always met with a quiet indifference. When she won the school's essay contest in eighth grade, the announcement had been made in the same monotone voice that was used to read off the lunch menu. When one of her white classmates won a similar contest the following year, the teachers threw a small party in the classroom to celebrate. Aisha had watched from her desk as the girl was handed a shiny certificate and a bouquet of flowers, while her own achievement had barely been acknowledged.

Those moments stuck with her, not because she needed recognition, but because of what they represented. It was as if, no matter what she did, no matter how hard she tried, she would never be seen as enough. She would never fully belong.

The lesson was reinforced again and again, in ways big and small. The way her teachers would praise her for being "so articulate" as if it was a surprise that she could speak well. The way her white classmates would ask if they could touch her hair, treating her as if she were some kind of exotic creature rather than a person. The way the police in their neighborhood seemed to view every young black boy as a potential threat, stopping them for "routine checks" that never seemed to happen in other parts of town.

For a long time, Aisha had tried to follow the rules her parents had laid out for her. She had tried to be polite, to stay out of trouble, to keep her head down and do what was expected of her. But the older she got, the more she realized that no matter how much she tried to fit in, there would always be a wall between her and the world that others moved through so easily.

One of the most profound lessons came when she was in high school. She had been nominated for a scholarship to attend a prestigious summer program at a nearby university. It was a big deal, only a few students from her school had ever been selected, and Aisha was excited about the opportunity. She had filled out the application, written the essay, and gotten glowing recommendations from her teachers.

But when the time came for the final decision, Aisha's application was mysteriously "lost." By the time the mistake was discovered, it was too late. The deadline had passed, and the opportunity was gone. She never got an explanation—just a shrug from the school counselor, who offered her a half-hearted apology.

It was then that Aisha realized something she had been resisting for a long time: the system wasn't just flawed, it was rigged. And it wasn't rigged in her favor.

That experience marked a turning point for her. It was no longer enough to keep her head down and hope for the best. The world wasn't going to give her the opportunities she deserved. She was going to have to take them, to fight for them, to demand what she had earned.

Aisha's childhood had been filled with lessons like lessons about power, about who had it and who didn't, about how the world was set up to keep people like her in their place. But those lessons didn't break her. If anything, they made her stronger. They fueled her determination to rise above the barriers that had been placed in her way, to prove that she was more than what the world expected of her.

Her family had taught her to survive, to navigate a world that was hostile and unforgiving. But Aisha wasn't interested in just surviving. She wanted more than that. She wanted to change the world that had taught her so many painful lessons.

As she reflected on her childhood, Aisha began to understand that the path she was on was not just about her. It was about all the kids who had grown up like her, who had learned the same harsh lessons, who had been told in a million subtle ways that they didn't belong. It was about her parents, who had done everything they could to protect her from a world they knew would never fully accept her. And it was about her grandmother, who had survived in a world far harsher than the one Aisha knew and had done so with pride and dignity.

Aisha didn't know exactly where her path would lead, but she knew that it was time to start walking it. The lessons from her childhood had shaped her, but they wouldn't define her. She would take what she had learned and use it to tear down the walls that had been built around her, the walls that had been built around her family for generations.

It was time to start fighting back.

Chapter 5: The System's Design

By the time Aisha reached her senior year of high school, she had developed a keen awareness of how the world worked—how it was built, and more importantly, who it was built for. The unspoken lessons of her childhood had crystallized into a clear understanding: the system wasn't broken. It was functioning exactly as it was designed to—just not for people like her.

The tipping point came one afternoon during history class, when her teacher, Mr. Barnes, was lecturing on the Civil Rights Movement. He stood at the front of the room, his voice droning on as he showed slides of Martin Luther King Jr., Rosa Parks, and the March on Washington. Aisha had always been interested in history, but the way it was taught in school made it seem like a distant memory, a chapter that had closed long ago.

"You see," Mr. Barnes said, pacing in front of the projector screen, "the Civil Rights Movement was a turning point in American history. It was the moment when racial equality became a priority in this country."

Aisha felt a knot tighten in her chest. She had heard this narrative before—the idea that the struggles of her ancestors had been neatly packaged into the past, with progress having been made, leaving the present free of the same injustices.

But when Mr. Barnes clicked to the next slide—a smiling photograph of a newly integrated school—Aisha couldn't stay silent any longer.

"Is that really true?" she blurted out, her voice sharper than she intended.

The class fell silent. Mr. Barnes paused mid-level, turning to face her with raised eyebrows. "Excuse me?"

"Racial equality—has that really been achieved?" Aisha continued, her words now spilling out. "Because it doesn't feel that way for people like me. It doesn't feel like the system has changed much at all."

A ripple of tension spread through the classroom. Some students looked down at their desks, while others shot Aisha curious or wary glances. Mr. Barnes cleared his throat, clearly unprepared for the challenge.

"Well," he began, adjusting his glasses, "we've made significant strides since then. Of course, there's still work to be done, but we live in a very different time now. The opportunities—"

"Opportunities?" Aisha interrupted. "Like the opportunity to go to a school where the books are falling apart, and we barely have enough teachers? Or the opportunity to be passed over for scholarships because of 'lost' applications? Or the opportunity to be followed around stores because people assume we're going to steal something?"

Mr. Barnes opened his mouth to respond, but Aisha didn't give him the chance.

"Civil rights weren't a finish line," she continued. "The system still treats us like we're less than—like we don't belong. And it's not just about laws. It's about how everything is set up to keep certain people on top, while the rest of us must fight just to get a seat at the table."

The room was dead silent now, the weight of Aisha's words hanging heavy in the air. Mr. Barnes shifted uncomfortably, clearly unsure how to respond. Finally, after a long pause, he spoke.

"I understand your frustration, Aisha, but you must recognize that we've made a lot of progress. You're sitting in this classroom, aren't you? That's a direct result of the efforts of the Civil Rights Movement."

Aisha felt a flash of anger. The implication that her mere presence in the room was somehow a gift, a product of the country's supposed progress, stung deeply.

"I'm here because I worked hard," she shot back. "Not because the system gave me anything."

Mr. Barnes was taken aback, but before he could respond, the bell rang, signaling the end of the period. The students quickly gathered their things and filed out of the classroom, leaving Aisha standing there, her heart pounding.

As she left the room, her head buzzing with frustration, Aisha realized something. For the first time, she had openly challenged the narrative that the world had been trying to sell her. The narrative that everything was fine now, that the fight was over, that people like her should be grateful for the "progress" that had been made.

But Aisha wasn't buying it. The more she looked around, the more she saw how the system had been designed to give the appearance of change while keeping the old structures of inequality firmly in place. The schools in her neighborhood were still underfunded. The job opportunities were still scarce. The police were still biased. And at the core of it all was a system that continued to privilege one group over another, maintaining the same divisions her grandmother had fought against decades ago.

It wasn't just about individual racism, although that certainly played a part. It was about how the institutions, the schools, the government, the police, the economy—were all built to maintain those divisions. Even when laws changed, the underlying structures didn't. They were designed to keep certain people at the bottom and others at the top. And unless those structures were dismantled, nothing would really change.

Aisha started paying closer attention to the world around her. She read articles about the wealth gap between black and white families, how decades of discriminatory housing policies had created entire communities of poverty. She learned about how school funding was tied to property taxes, meaning that wealthier neighborhoods had better schools, while neighborhoods like hers were left with crumbling buildings and outdated textbooks.

She saw how the justice system disproportionately targeted black and brown people, how the media portrayed people of color as criminals, reinforcing the stereotypes that kept people afraid of them. She watched as politicians passed laws that seemed to help the surface but did little to address the root causes of inequality.

Aisha's eyes were opening to the bigger picture. The system wasn't just unfair, but intentional. It had been built this way, piece by piece, to ensure that the status quo remained. And that realization filled her with both anger and determination.

One night, after dinner, Aisha sat down with her father at the kitchen table. She had been thinking about this conversation for days, unsure of how to start, but knowing she couldn't stay silent anymore.

"Dad," she began, her voice careful, "why did you always tell me to keep my head down? I mean, I understand wanting to stay safe, but... don't you think that's part of the problem? That we've been told to just accept things the way they are?"

Her father looked at her, his face lined with years of worry and hard work. He sighed deeply and leaned back in his chair.

"It's not about accepting it," he said quietly. "It's about surviving. I've seen what happens when people push too hard, when they try to change things. I didn't want that for you. I didn't want you to get hurt."

Aisha nodded, understanding where her father was coming from, but still feeling the fire inside her.

"I get that, Dad. But I'm not okay with just surviving. I want to do more than that. I want to change things. And I think I can."

Her father was silent for a moment, his eyes searching her face. Finally, he nodded, though his expression remained somber.

"I know you can," he said softly. "But it's a hard road. Just... be careful."

Aisha knew he was right—it would be a hard road. But she also knew that it was the only road she could take. She couldn't live with the knowledge that the system was rigged and do nothing about it. The system had been designed to keep her in her place, but she wasn't going to stay there.

It was time to start finding ways to tear it down.

Chapter 6: The Silent Rules

There were rules in place that nobody talked about, but everybody seemed to understand. They weren't written down in textbooks or posted on billboards, but they were enforced as strictly as any law. These were the rules that told Aisha and people like her where they could go, how they should act, and, more importantly, how they should stay in their place.

Growing up, Aisha had sensed these rules long before she could name them. They were the invisible boundaries that separated her neighborhood from the wealthier parts of town. They were the reasons her family never ate at certain restaurants or shopped at certain stores. And they were the same rules that dictated how people treated her, how they looked at her, and what they expected her to be.

In school, the silent rules were everywhere. They dictated who sat with whom at lunch, who got invited to which parties, and even which clubs and sports teams were "for them." The lines were clear: white kids belonged on the swim team, while kids like Aisha gravitated toward track. There were always a few exceptions—white kids who joined the track team and black kids who swam—but everyone knew those exceptions were just that: exceptions. And if anyone broke those unspoken rules, they were quietly but firmly pushed back into place.

The silent rules weren't enforced through explicit racism, at least not most of the time. Instead, they worked through subtle cues, like the way white students shifted uncomfortably if Aisha joined their conversation, or how teachers expected her to speak on behalf of "her people" whenever race came up in class discussions. It was in the way they praised her for being "so well-spoken," as if they had expected her to be otherwise. It was in the way she could feel eyes on her when she walked into a room, waiting for her to say or do something that would confirm their assumptions about her.

The rules were also evident in her interactions with authority figures—police officers, store clerks, even teachers. There was always a sense that she was being watched more closely than others, that she had to be extra careful not to make any mistakes, because her mistakes would be judged more harshly. She had learned from a young age to keep her head down when walking past the police, to avoid being "too loud" in public spaces, to be extra polite in stores so no one would accuse her of something she hadn't done.

Aisha had been taught these rules by her parents, who had been taught them by theirs. It wasn't that they believed the rules were right, it was that they knew the consequences of breaking them. The silent rules were there to maintain the status quo, to keep certain people in their place, and breaking them often came with a price.

One afternoon, Aisha found herself at the local mall with her best friend, Simone. They had spent the day window shopping, saving up their money to buy a few small things. It had been a good day, the kind of day that made Aisha feel like, just for a moment, she could forget about the silent rules that governed her life.

But as they entered a high-end clothing store, the weight of those rules came crashing back. Almost immediately, they felt the eyes of the store clerk on them, following their every move. Aisha and Simone exchanged a glance but said nothing, both accustomed to the feeling of being watched.

"Can I help you?" the clerk asked, her tone laced with suspicion as she walked over, her eyes flicking up and down at them as though they didn't belong.

"We're just looking," Simone said, her voice polite but firm.

The clerk lingered for a moment longer, her eyes narrowing slightly before she turned and walked away. But even after she was gone, Aisha could feel the tension in the air. Every step they took felt like it was being scrutinized, every glance at a price tag was met with the assumption that they couldn't afford what they were looking at. It was the silent rule that said people like them didn't shop in stores like this. They were expected to stay in their lane, to get to know their place.

Aisha had felt this many times before, but today something about it felt more infuriating. She was tired of being followed in stores, tired of the assumption that she was up to no good, tired of living under the weight of these silent rules that everyone seemed to know but no one ever acknowledged.

As they left the store, Simone shook her head in frustration. "I hate when they do that," she muttered. "Like we're going to steal something just because we're here."

"Yeah, it's ridiculous," Aisha agreed, but her mind was already racing ahead, thinking about all the other ways these rules showed up in her life, all the ways they shaped her interactions with the world.

Later that night, Aisha sat at her desk, trying to focus on her homework, but her thoughts kept drifting back to the silent rules. The ones that told her she had to be twice as good to get half as much. The ones that said she had to smile and be polite, no matter how much disrespect she encountered. The ones that kept people like her boxed in constantly reminded that they didn't quite belong.

But the more Aisha thought about it, the more she realized that these rules were just another way of controlling people, of maintaining the systems of power that had always been in place. The silent rules weren't just about individual behavior—they were about upholding the larger structures that kept certain groups at the top and others at the bottom.

It wasn't just about being watched in stores. It was about being watched in life—constantly under surveillance, constantly having to prove that she was worthy of the space she occupied. The silent rules worked to keep her, and people like her in a state of constant vigilance, always aware that any misstep could lead to serious consequences.

The silent rules were insidious because they were so easy to internalize. Over time, people started to police themselves, to limit their own actions, to stay in their place without needing to be told. And that was exactly how the system was designed to work. If people believed that breaking the rules wasn't worth the risk, they would stop trying to break them at all.

But Aisha wasn't willing to accept that anymore. She wasn't willing to live her life according to rules that were designed to keep her down. She wasn't willing to keep quiet, to stay small, to follow the path that had been laid out for her.

It was time to start breaking the rules—not in the ways the system expected, by acting out in anger or rebellion, but by refusing to play the game altogether. It was time to challenge the assumptions that underpinned the system, to question why the rules existed in the first place, and to fight back against the forces that tried to keep her in her place.

Aisha didn't have all the answers yet, but she knew one thing for sure: the silent rules might be powerful, but they weren't unbreakable. And she was ready to start breaking them.

Chapter 7: Voices of Dissent

As the months passed, Aisha found herself increasingly drawn to people who, like her, were beginning to see the world for what it really was. She had always known, in some small way, that the system was rigged, but now that realization burned like a fire inside her. She couldn't go back to the way things were—to staying silent, to keeping her head down, to pretending that everything was fine. And she wasn't alone.

The first person she really connected with was Jason, a senior who sat a few rows behind her in history class. Jason was quiet but observant, always paying close attention during discussions, especially when it came to topics about inequality and justice. He rarely spoke up, but when he did, his words carried weight. He had a way of cutting through the noise and getting straight to the heart of the matter.

Aisha had noticed him before, but it wasn't until one afternoon after class that they talked. She had stayed behind to ask Mr. Barnes a question, but as soon as she left the classroom, Jason was waiting in the hallway, leaning casually against the lockers.

"You were right, you know," he said as she walked by, his voice low and calm.

Aisha stopped, turning to look at him. "About what?"

"About what you said the other day," Jason replied, pushing off the locker and standing upright. "About the Civil Rights Movement and how it didn't magically fix everything. You're right—people like to act like it's all in the past, but the truth is, nothing's really changed."

Aisha blinked, surprised that someone had not only been paying attention but agreed with her. Most of the time, it felt like she was shouting into a void.

"Thanks," she said, unsure of what else to say.

Jason shrugged. "It's the truth. People don't want to hear it, but it's the truth."

For a moment, they stood in silence, the buzz of students rushing through the hallway fading into the background. There was something about Jason's presence that felt solid, grounded—like he understood what she was feeling without her having to explain it.

"Have you ever heard of the local activist group?" Jason asked after a beat.

Aisha shook her head. "No, what is it?"

"There's a group of people—mostly students, but some older folks too—who've been organizing around stuff like this. Protesting, raising awareness, trying to push for real change in the community. I think you'd be into it."

Aisha's interest was piqued. "What kind of things do they do?"

"They've been fighting for better funding for schools, more accountability for the police, that kind of thing. It's small right now, but they're making waves."

Aisha felt her pulse quicken. This was exactly what she had been looking for—people who weren't just talking about the problem but actively trying to change it.

"Do you go to the meetings?" she asked.

Jason nodded. "Yeah, I've been going for a few months now. You should come to the next one. They meet at the community center every Thursday night."

For the first time in a long while, Aisha felt a sense of hope. There were others out there who saw the same problems she did, who were willing to stand up and do something about it. Maybe she didn't have to do this alone.

"I'll think about it," she said, trying to keep her voice casual, though inside, she was already planning to attend.

Jason gave her a small smile. "You should. We need more voices like yours."

That Thursday night, Aisha found herself standing outside the community center, feeling a mix of excitement and nerves. She had never been involved in anything like this before. The idea of speaking up, of standing alongside others who were fighting back, thrilled her. But it also made her anxious. What if she didn't belong? What if she wasn't radical enough or knowledgeable enough? What if these people didn't take her seriously?

Pushing those doubts aside, she took a deep breath and walked inside.

The room was small but filled with energy. There were about twenty people scattered around, some sitting in a circle of folding chairs, others leaning against the walls, talking in small groups. The atmosphere was casual but focused, like everyone was there with a purpose. Aisha immediately spotted Jason sitting with a group near the front. When he saw her, he waved her over.

"Glad you made it," he said as she sat down next to him.

"Yeah, me too," Aisha replied, her eyes scanning the room.

The meeting began with introductions. Each person shared a bit about themselves and why they had joined the group. Aisha listened closely as people talked about their frustrations with the education system, their experiences with police harassment, and their anger at the way the local government seemed to ignore their needs. It was like hearing her own thoughts spoken aloud, by people from different walks of life but with the same underlying frustrations.

When it was her turn to introduce herself, Aisha hesitated for a moment. But then, as she looked around at the faces of people who were there for the same reasons she was, she felt a surge of confidence.

"My name's Aisha," she began, her voice steady. "And I'm tired of pretending that things are getting better when they're not. I'm tired of watching my family, my friends, and my community struggle while people who have power look the other way. I'm here because I want to do something about it."

A few people nodded, and one woman in her twenties gave Aisha an encouraging smile. "That's why we're all here," the woman said. "Welcome to the group."

As the meeting went on, Aisha felt more and more at home. They discussed upcoming protests, strategies for raising awareness, and ways to pressure local officials to listen to their demands. It wasn't just talk—it was action. These people weren't waiting for change to happen. They were making it happen.

After the meeting ended, Aisha stayed behind to talk with Jason and a few others. There was a lot to learn—about the history of activism in their community, about how to organize effectively, about how to navigate the dangers that came with challenging the system. But for the first time, Aisha felt like she was part of something bigger than herself. She wasn't just a bystander anymore. She was becoming a voice of dissent.

Over the next few weeks, Aisha became more involved in the group. She attended protests, helped plan events, and even started speaking at public forums. The more she did, the more her confidence grew. She began to see herself as a leader, someone who could inspire others to speak out and fight back.

One evening, after a particularly intense protest where the police had shown up in riot gear, Aisha sat with Jason on the steps of the community center, the adrenaline still coursing through her veins.

"I never thought I'd be doing this," she admitted, looking out at the empty street. "I used to think that fighting back wouldn't make a difference."

Jason nodded; his expression thoughtful. "A lot of people feel that way. But we must keep pushing. Even if it feels like we're not getting anywhere, every action we take chips away at the system. We might not see the change overnight, but we're planting the seeds."

Aisha thought about that—about the idea of planting seeds for a future she might never fully see. It was a heavy thought, but it also gave her a sense of purpose. She wasn't just fighting for herself. She was fighting for everyone who came after her, for the next generation who would grow up in a world that she hoped would be better than the one she had inherited.

That night, as Aisha lay in bed, she felt a quiet sense of determination settle over her. She had found her voice, and she wasn't going to let it be silenced. The system was designed to keep people like her quiet, to make them feel powerless, but she wasn't powerless anymore.

She had found her place among the voices of dissent. And together, they were going to tear down the walls that had been built to keep them in their place.

Chapter 8: Public vs. Private Hate

As Aisha became more involved in activism, she started to see the world in sharper focus. The truths she had always known—the ones that had simmered just beneath the surface of her life—were now laid bare. She was learning to name the forces that had shaped her experiences and the experiences of her community. But what became increasingly clear was the difference between the hatred that was shown out in the open and the kind that festered behind closed doors.

Public hate was easy to spot. It was loud, aggressive, and often violent. It showed itself in the way the police responded to protests—riot gear, batons, and tear gas, even when the demonstrations were peaceful. It was in the slurs hurled at her and the other protesters by counter demonstrators, faces twisted in anger as they shouted things like "Go back where you came from!" and "You people are the problem!" The rawness of that kind of hate was undeniable, and it came with a sense of clarity. There was no pretending it didn't exist. No one could ignore it when it was thrown in their face.

Aisha had experienced public hate before, but now she was seeing it on a new level. During one protest outside city hall, things had escalated quickly. The group had been demanding accountability for a recent incident where police had used excessive force on a young black man. They chanted for justice, holding signs that read "Black Lives Matter" and "No Justice, No Peace." But soon, the counter-protesters arrived—mostly older white men, with a smattering of younger faces, all of them seething with anger.

"You're the reason there's crime in this city!" one of them shouted, spitting in their direction.

Aisha watched as the police formed a line between the two groups, but their presence didn't make her feel safe. If anything, it made her feel more vulnerable. She knew whose side the police were on, and it wasn't hers. The tension in the air was thick, almost suffocating, as the insults flew back and forth. A few of the counter-protesters carried Confederate flags, a stark reminder of the legacy of hate that had shaped the world they lived in.

At one point, a man broke through the police line and lunged toward the protesters, grabbing at a sign and tearing it in half. The crowd surged, and for a moment, it looked like a fight was going to break out. But the police quickly moved in, pushing the man back toward the other side. He left with a smirk on his face, as if he had proven something.

It was moments like this that made the hatred so tangible, so impossible to ignore. Aisha could feel it in the way people looked at her, in the venom in their voices, in the violence that simmered just beneath the surface. Public hate was brutal, but it was also something she could confront head-on. It was in the open, where she could see it and fight back.

But then there was the other kind of hate—the quiet kind. The kind that didn't announce itself with slurs or fists but was just as insidious. This was the private hate, the kind that lingered in boardrooms and classrooms, in polite conversations and friendly smiles. It was harder to pin down, but it was just as damaging.

Aisha first became acutely aware of this form of hate when she and her activist group started pushing for changes in their school district. They were advocating for better funding for the schools in their neighborhoods, for more equitable resources, and for a curriculum that included more accurate representations of black history and culture. On paper, it seemed like a reasonable request. Who could argue against better schools and fair representation?

But the resistance they encountered was subtle. When they presented their demands to the school board, they were met with tight smiles and nodding heads. The board members listened politely, thanked them for their time, and promised to "look into it." But nothing happened. Weeks went by, then months, and every time Aisha and her group followed up, they were given excuses. "We're reviewing the budget." "We're looking for ways to accommodate your requests." "These things take time."

It became clear that the school board had no intention of making any real changes. They were more concerned with maintaining the status quo than with addressing the systemic inequalities that Aisha and her friends were fighting against. And yet, they never said it outright. There were no angry outbursts or racist comments. Just a quiet, polite refusal to engage with the real issues.

This was the private hate, the kind that hid behind bureaucracy and pleasantries, the kind that never raised its voice but still managed to shut people like Aisha out. It was the same kind of hate that kept certain neighborhoods poor, that kept black families from getting loans for better homes, that ensured schools in white neighborhoods got more funding. It was a system of exclusion disguised as professionalism.

Aisha saw this private hate most clearly one afternoon when she went to a city planning meeting with Jason and a few others from the group. They were there to advocate for more affordable housing in the city, as rising rents were forcing many black families out of their homes. The meeting was full of local business leaders, developers, and city officials. It was a different crowd than the ones at the protests—no angry shouting, no slurs. Everyone was dressed in suits and business attire, speaking in calm, measured tones.

When it was time for public comment, Aisha stepped up to the podium and made her case. She spoke about the displacement of black families, about how the lack of affordable housing was pushing people out of their communities and making it harder for them to stay connected to their support systems. She was clear and articulate, laying out the facts and calling for action.

But when she finished, the response she got was chilling in its calmness. One of the developers stood up, adjusting his glasses, and smiled. "We appreciate your concerns," he said, his voice smooth and patronizing. "But we must be realistic about what's possible. These projects take time, and there are a lot of factors at play. We're doing everything we can to address the housing crisis, but there are no easy solutions."

Aisha could feel the dismissiveness in his tone, even though he hadn't said anything overtly offensive. He was telling her, in the politest way possible, that her concerns didn't matter. The room was full of nodding heads, people who agreed with him, people who would go on with their lives without ever giving a second thought to the families being pushed out of their homes.

It was in that moment that Aisha truly understood the power of private hate. It was the kind that allowed people to feel like they were doing the right thing, even as they upheld systems that perpetuated inequality. It was the kind of hate that didn't need to shout or throw punches because it worked through exclusion, through denial, through making sure that people like her were kept on the outside, looking in.

As Aisha left the meeting that day, she felt a new kind of anger boiling inside her. The public hate was brutal, but it was honest. The people who yelled at her on the streets made it clear where they stood. But this private hate—the one hidden behind smiles and polite words—was more dangerous because it pretended to be something it wasn't. It pretended to be reasonable, fair, even compassionate, all while working to maintain the very systems that kept people like her oppressed.

Aisha knew that if she was going to keep fighting, she would have to learn how to confront both kinds of hate. The public hate required strength and resilience in the face of aggression. But the private hate required something else—strategy, persistence, and the ability to see through the facade of politeness that so often disguised the real barriers to change.

The next time she spoke at a meeting, she would be ready.

Chapter 9: Cultural Misunderstandings

As Aisha continued her journey into activism, she began to realize that not all obstacles came from direct opposition or outright hatred. Sometimes, the most frustrating moments came from those who claimed to be on her side—people who believed they were allies but whose lack of understanding perpetuated the very systems they thought they were fighting against. These encounters, filled with well-meaning ignorance, were often more difficult to navigate than the obvious hatred she faced from her detractors.

It was during one of the group's weekly meetings that Aisha first encountered this kind of misunderstanding. A young woman named Emily, one of the few white members of the group, had been attending meetings for a few weeks. Emily was well-meaning and eager to help, but her enthusiasm often bordered on condescension, as though she believed she knew better than the people who were directly impacted by the issues they were fighting against.

That evening, the group was discussing their next steps in advocating for better school funding. Several members of the group, including Aisha, were frustrated by the lack of response from the school board and were brainstorming ways to apply more pressure. They talked about organizing a protest outside the next board meeting, reaching out to local media, and gathering testimonies from students and parents affected by the school's lack of resources.

Emily, who had been quietly taking notes, suddenly raised her hand. "I think we should focus on creating a more positive message," she suggested, her voice bright and confident. "Instead of focusing on what's wrong with the system, maybe we should show how far we've come and highlight the progress that's been made. People don't like feeling attacked, and if we make the message more optimistic, it might inspire more people to support us."

Aisha felt her stomach tighten. She had heard this kind of sentiment before—the idea that, in order to be heard, people like her had to frame their struggles in a way that made others feel comfortable, that they had to be polite in their demands for basic rights. It was as though they were expected to be grateful for the scraps of progress that had been made, rather than demanding the full measure of justice they deserved.

Before Aisha could respond, Jason leaned forward, frowning. "Emily, I get what you're saying, but we've been trying the 'positive' route for months now. It hasn't gotten us anywhere. The school board doesn't care how nice we are or how optimistic we make our message—they care about keeping their budget intact and maintaining the status quo."

Emily looked taken aback, clearly surprised by Jason's response. "I just think we should be careful not to alienate people. If we come across as too angry or demanding, they'll just tune us out."

Aisha had heard enough. She knew Emily meant well, but her words felt like a slap in the face. It wasn't about being "too angry" or "too demanding"—it was about being heard at all. For so long, people like Aisha had been forced to soften their voices, to make their pain palatable, so that those in power could remain comfortable.

"Emily," Aisha said, her voice steady but firm, "I get that you're trying to help, but you need to understand something. When you tell us to focus on a 'positive' message, what you're really saying is that we should water down our truth to make it easier for people to hear. But the truth is ugly. It's uncomfortable. And we can't keep pretending that everything is fine just to avoid making people feel guilty or uneasy."

Emily's eyes widened, clearly not expecting the pushback. "That's not what I meant," she stammered. "I just thought—"

"I know what you meant," Aisha interrupted, her tone softening slightly. "And I know you're coming from a good place. But this isn't about making people feel good. It's about demanding real change. And sometimes, that means making people uncomfortable."

The room was silent for a moment, the weight of Aisha's words hanging in the air. Emily nodded slowly, looking down at her hands. "I'm sorry," she said quietly. "I didn't mean to undermine what you're saying. I just... I didn't think about it that way."

Aisha offered her a small smile, grateful that Emily was willing to listen. "It's okay. But this is the reality we live in every day. It's not enough to talk about progress—we need to talk about what's still broken, because if we don't, nothing will ever change."

After that meeting, Aisha found herself thinking more about the well-meaning but often misguided attempts by people like Emily to help. They weren't bad people, and many of them genuinely wanted to make a difference. But their lack of lived experience meant they didn't fully understand the depth of the problems they were trying to solve. They didn't know what it was like to live under the weight of systemic oppression, to have your voice silenced or ignored, to be told that your anger was unjustified or your demands unreasonable.

In the weeks that followed, Aisha encountered more of these cultural misunderstandings. During one protest, a local reporter interviewed her about the group's demands. He was polite enough, but as the conversation went on, it became clear that he didn't really grasp the nuances of what they were fighting for.

"So, would you say this is mostly about improving the schools in your neighborhood?" the reporter asked, his tone sympathetic but shallow.

"It's about more than that," Aisha explained, trying to keep her frustration in check. "The schools are just one piece of a much larger problem. It's about housing, healthcare, job opportunities—all the things that are systematically denied to black and brown communities. The schools are failing because the system is failing us."

The reporter nodded, but Aisha could tell he wasn't really getting it. "Right, right. But don't you think that focusing on the schools is a more achievable goal? You know, something more... manageable?"

Aisha clenched her jaw, trying to find the right words. She understood what the reporter was doing—trying to simplify the story, to make it digestible for his audience. But in doing so, he was erasing the full scope of what they were fighting for. It wasn't just about making one small fix; it was about dismantling a system that had been designed to keep people like her at the margins.

"We can't afford to think small," Aisha said finally, her voice steady. "If we only focus on one part of the problem, we're not really solving anything. We must look at the whole system and how it's all connected."

The reporter nodded again, scribbling in his notebook. But Aisha wasn't sure he really understood what she was saying.

These moments of cultural misunderstanding, while frustrating, helped Aisha refine her message. She realized that part of the fight wasn't just against the system itself, but against the narratives that surrounded it—the narratives that reduced their struggles to single-issue causes, or that framed their demands in a way that made them easier for others to accept.

It wasn't just about educating the oppressors; it was about educating the allies, too—people like Emily and the well-meaning reporter, who wanted to help but didn't fully understand the complexities of the issues they were trying to address. Aisha knew she couldn't expect everyone to get it right away, but she also knew that true allyship required more than just good intentions. It required listening, learning, and being willing to confront uncomfortable truths.

The next time Emily spoke up in a meeting, Aisha noticed a shift. Instead of jumping in with her own suggestions, Emily listened. She took a step back, letting the people who had lived these experiences lead the conversation. And when she did speak, it was with a newfound humility, a recognition that being an ally meant following the leadership of those who had been fighting these battles their entire lives.

Aisha knew there would be more misunderstandings, more moments where well-meaning people tried to soften the message or narrow the focus. But she also knew that these conversations were part of the process. Change wasn't going to happen overnight, and not everyone was going to get it right on the first try. What mattered was that people were willing to learn, to grow, and to push past their own discomfort in order to stand in solidarity with those on the frontlines of the fight.

And if people like Emily were willing to listen, Aisha was willing to keep talking.

Chapter 10: Normalization of Hatred

Hatred, Aisha realized, wasn't just something that lived in the hearts of a few angry people. It wasn't just the slurs hurled at her during protests or the suspicious glances she received in upscale stores. It wasn't always loud, violent, or obvious. Often, it was subtle, woven into the very fabric of society in such a way that it went unnoticed by those who benefited from it. Over time, it had become normalized—an accepted part of the world she lived in, something people learned to live with, rather than fight against.

Aisha first recognized the normalization of hatred when she began reflecting on her own life. For years, she had accepted the way things were without question. She had been told to keep her head down, to avoid making waves, to be grateful for the opportunities she had, even if they were limited. And for a long time, she had done exactly that. She had followed the unspoken rules, internalizing the idea that some doors would always be closed to her, that she didn't belong in certain spaces.

It was only now, after months of activism and self-reflection, that Aisha realized how deeply she had absorbed these messages. She had been taught, implicitly, to accept less—to expect less—because that was the way things were. And it wasn't just her. She saw it everywhere, in her community, in her family, in the way people navigated their lives with a quiet resignation, as though they had come to terms with the idea that the system wasn't designed for them.

Hatred had become so normalized that people barely even noticed it anymore. It was in the way black and brown neighborhoods were left to crumble, the streets filled with potholes, the schools underfunded, the grocery stores few and far between. It was in the way police patrolled those same neighborhoods with a heavy hand, their presence less about protection and more about control. It was in the way people like her were expected to be grateful for whatever scraps of progress had been made, even when that progress fell far short of what was needed.

One day, Aisha was walking through her neighborhood with her younger brother, Malik. He was twelve years old, and already, Aisha could see the world shaping him in ways she had hoped to protect him from. He had always been bright and curious, but lately, Aisha had noticed a hard-edge creeping into his demeanor, a wariness that hadn't been there before. It broke her heart to see it.

As they walked, Malik kicked a loose rock down the cracked sidewalk. "Why do they hate us so much?" he asked suddenly, his voice low and serious.

Aisha's heart sank. She had known this question would come one day, but she wasn't prepared for it. How could she explain something so complicated, something so deeply ingrained in the world around them?

"They don't all hate us," Aisha said softly, trying to find the right words. "But the system we live in—it was built to keep us down. It's been that way for a long time."

"But why?" Malik pressed, his eyes filled with confusion and hurt. "Why can't they just leave us alone?"

Aisha stopped walking and looked down at her brother, her chest tight with the weight of his question. She wanted to tell him that things would get better, that the world wasn't as bad as it seemed, but she couldn't lie to him. She couldn't sugarcoat the truth.

"People are scared of change," she said finally. "They're scared of losing control, of losing power. And when people are scared, they do things that don't make sense. They build systems that keep others down so they can stay on top."

Malik frowned, kicking the rock again. "That's stupid."

Aisha smiled, despite the heaviness in her heart. "Yeah, it is."

They walked in silence for a while, the weight of the conversation lingering between them. Aisha couldn't help but feel a sense of sadness. Malik was so young, and yet, he was already learning the same lessons she had learned at his age—the lesson that the world wasn't fair, that the odds were stacked against them, that they would have to work twice as hard just to be seen as equal.

As they passed by a row of boarded-up houses, Aisha thought about how easy it was for people outside their community to ignore what was happening here. For them, this wasn't their reality. They didn't have to live in neighborhoods where the schools were falling apart, where the air was thick with pollution, where opportunities were scarce. For them, the struggles of people like Aisha and Malik were something they saw on the news, something distant, disconnected from their own lives.

And because it wasn't their reality, it was easy for them to accept it as just the way things were. They could go about their lives, enjoying the benefits of a system that worked for them, without ever questioning why it worked that way or who it was hurting. They could tell themselves that the problems in neighborhoods like Aisha's were the result of bad choices or bad luck, rather than the direct result of decades of systemic oppression.

Aisha realized that this was how hatred became normalized. It wasn't just in the loud, obvious acts of racism. It was in the quiet acceptance of a broken system; in the way people turned a blind eye to injustice because it didn't affect them. It was in the way people shrugged and said, "That's just the way things are," as though they had no power to change it.

That night, Aisha sat at her desk, thinking about the conversation she had had with Malik. She couldn't stop thinking about how deeply the normalization of hatred had seeped into every aspect of their lives. It was so pervasive that even people in her own community had started to accept it. They had been taught to believe that they didn't deserve more, that they had to be content with the scraps they were given.

The next morning, Aisha attended a city council meeting with her activist group. They had been pushing for months to get the council to address the issue of police violence in their neighborhood, but every time they brought it up, they were met with the same dismissive responses.

"The police are just doing their job," one council member had said at a previous meeting. "We all want to feel safe, and the police are here to keep order."

It was the same argument every time—order and safety. But Aisha knew that what they really meant was control. They weren't interested in keeping people like her safe. They were interested in keeping people like her in line.

As she sat in the meeting, listening to the council members drone on about budgets and public safety, Aisha felt a familiar frustration rise within her. The system was designed to protect the people in power, and everyone else was expected to accept it. This was how hatred continued to thrive—through policies and practices that were cloaked in the language of "safety" and "order," but that were about maintaining control over marginalized communities.

When it was time for public comment, Aisha stood up. She had spoken at these meetings before, but today felt different. Today, she wasn't just speaking for herself—she was speaking for Malik, for her community, for everyone who had been taught to believe that this was the best they could hope for.

"We're tired of being told to accept the way things are," Aisha said, her voice steady but filled with conviction. "We're tired of being told that this is just the way the system works, that we should be grateful for what we have. The truth is the system doesn't work for us. It was never designed to work for us. And we're not going to accept that anymore."

The room was silent as Aisha spoke, her words cutting through the usual bureaucratic chatter. She could feel the weight of the moment, the power of her own voice. She wasn't asking for permission anymore. She was demanding change.

"We deserve better," Aisha continued, her eyes scanning the faces of the council members. "Our community deserves better. And we're not going to stop fighting until we get it."

When she finished, the room erupted in quiet murmurs. Some of the council members looked uncomfortable, shifting in their seats. Others simply nodded, as though they had heard it all before.

But Aisha didn't care. She wasn't speaking for them. She was speaking for the people who had been told for too long that they didn't deserve more. She was speaking for herself, for her brother, for her family, for everyone who had learned to live with a system that was built on hatred.

Walking out of the meeting, Aisha felt a sense of clarity. The fight was far from over, but she knew what she was up against now. Hatred had been normalized for so long that people didn't even recognize it anymore. But Aisha did. And she wasn't going to let it continue.

The next step was figuring out how to tear down the walls that had been built so carefully, so quietly, to keep people like her in their place. It wouldn't be easy, but Aisha had never been ready for the fight.

Chapter 11: Whispers in the Shadows

Aisha had always known the fight for justice wouldn't be easy. But as she became more involved in the movement, she started to realize just how deeply entrenched the system really was. There were the obvious obstacles—police brutality, underfunded schools, housing discrimination—but there were also forces operating behind the scenes, quietly working to maintain the status quo. These forces didn't march in the streets or shout at protests. They operated in whispers, in closed-door meetings, in decisions made far from the public eye. It was here, in the shadows, that some of the most powerful resistance to change took place.

One evening, Aisha sat with Jason and the rest of the activist group, going over their next steps in the fight for police accountability. They had managed to get the city council to agree to a public forum on the issue, a small but significant victory. But Jason had learned through a contact that the police union had been quietly lobbying behind the scenes to limit any real reforms. The public forum, it seemed, was just for show.

"They're doing everything they can to undermine us," Jason said, his face tense as he leaned over the table. "The union's been meeting with council members, trying to water down any meaningful changes. They'll let us have our say in public, but they're already making sure nothing actually happens."

Aisha felt a surge of frustration. She had suspected that something like this was happening, but hearing it confirmed made her blood boil. "So what do we do?" she asked. "How do we fight back if they're already making deals behind closed doors?"

Jason looked at her, his expression grim. "We expose them. We need to shine a light on what they're doing, make it clear that they're working against the will of the people. The problem is, it's hard to prove. They're careful not to leave a trail."

Aisha leaned back in her chair, her mind racing. It was infuriating, knowing that even when they won a public battle, the real fight was happening where they couldn't see it. This wasn't just about protesting in the streets or speaking at public meetings—it was about uncovering the hidden mechanisms of power that were actively working against them.

It wasn't long before Aisha got a firsthand glimpse of these shadowy forces. A few days later, she received an unexpected call from an anonymous number. When she answered, a deep voice on the other end of the line told her to meet at a coffee shop across town, away from the neighborhoods where she was known. There, the voice said, she would learn something important.

Aisha was hesitant, but her curiosity got the better of her. She knew it could be a trap, or just someone trying to scare her. But she also knew that if there was a chance to learn more about the forces working against them, she had to take it.

When she arrived at the coffee shop, she saw a man sitting alone in the corner, a baseball cap pulled low over his face. As soon as she approached, he gestured for her to sit down.

"I don't have much time," the man said, his voice low and gravelly. "But you need to know what's going on behind the scenes."

Aisha sat down cautiously, her heart pounding. "Who are you?"

"That's not important," he replied, glancing around the room as if making sure no one was watching. "What's important is that the people you're fighting are bigger than you think. The police union, the council—there's more to it. There are business leaders in this city who benefit from keeping things the way they are. They're the ones funding the campaigns of the council members who oppose you. They're the ones making sure the police stay well-funded, no matter what."

Aisha felt a chill run down her spine. She had suspected that powerful people were working behind the scenes, but hearing it laid out so plainly was unsettling.

"Why are you telling me this?" she asked, her voice barely above a whisper.

"Because I believe in what you're doing," the man said, his eyes meeting hers for the first time. "I've seen what happens when people like you get too close to the truth. They'll try to discredit you, make you look like radicals, like you're asking for too much. But they're the ones with everything to lose if you succeed. The people in power—business owners, developers, politicians—they need things to stay the way they are. And they're willing to do whatever it takes to keep it that way."

Aisha's mind was spinning. She had always known that systemic change was hard, but this was a whole new level of opposition. It wasn't just the police or the city council they were up against. It was the people who profited from the system itself—people who had the money and influence to quietly pull the strings behind the scenes.

"What can we do?" Aisha asked, her voice urgent. "How do we fight back if we can't even see who's really in control?"

The man leaned in closer. "You expose them. You show the public what's really going on. You make noise, and you don't stop until people start paying attention. But you must be careful. These people don't like being exposed. They'll try to turn the public against you, make you look like the bad guys. You must be smarter than them."

Before Aisha could ask any more questions, the man stood up. "I've told you all I can. Be careful."

And with that, he walked out of the coffee shop, leaving Aisha sitting alone, her heart racing and her mind filled with questions.

That night, Aisha couldn't stop thinking about the conversation. She knew that the man's warning wasn't just paranoia. She had seen it before—the way the media sometimes twisted their protests, the way public officials downplayed their demands as "radical" or "unrealistic." Now she understood that it was all part of a larger strategy—a strategy designed to keep people like her from getting too close to the real centers of power.

The next morning, Aisha met with Jason and the rest of the group to share what she had learned. They were all quiet as she relayed the conversation, the weight of the information settling over them like a heavy blanket.

"So they're using money to keep us quiet," Jason said, leaning back in his chair, his jaw clenched. "I should've known."

Aisha nodded. "It's not just about the police. It's about the entire system. There are people with a lot to lose if we succeed, and they're doing everything they can to make sure we don't."

For a long moment, no one spoke. The reality of the situation was daunting. It was one thing to fight against visible forces, like the police or the city council. But how could they fight back against people they couldn't even see—people who operated in the shadows, pulling the strings without ever stepping into the light?

"We need to start digging," Aisha said finally, her voice resolute. "We need to find out who these people are. If they're funding the council members who oppose us, we need to make that public. If they're benefiting from keeping our neighborhoods underfunded, we need to show the world. The more we expose them, the harder it'll be for them to keep hiding."

The group agreed, and over the next few weeks, they began their investigation. It wasn't easy. The forces working against them were careful, leaving little trace of their influence. But Aisha and her friends were relentless. They dug through public records, followed the money, and slowly began to piece together a picture of who was really pulling the strings.

What they found was both infuriating and unsurprising. Several of the city's most prominent business leaders were funneling money into the campaigns of the council members who opposed police reform. These same business leaders had a vested interest in keeping the police well-funded and heavily involved in the "protection" of their businesses—especially as the city became more gentrified and working-class families were pushed out of their neighborhoods.

The more they uncovered, the clearer it became: the fight for justice wasn't just about changing laws or policies. It was about dismantling a system that was deeply intertwined with money and power. The people in charge weren't just maintaining the status quo out of ignorance or complacency—they were actively benefiting from it. And they would do whatever it took to protect their interests.

One evening, after weeks of digging, the group gathered to review their findings. Aisha felt a mixture of anger and determination as she looked at the evidence they had collected. They had names, financial records, and proof of the backroom deals that were being made to silence their movement.

"We need to make this public," Jason said, his voice steady. "People need to see what's really going on."

Aisha nodded. "We will. But we have to be smart about it. If we go public with this, they're going to come after us. We need to be ready for whatever they throw our way."

The group agreed, and together, they began planning their next move. They would expose the hidden forces working against them, but they wouldn't stop there. They would keep pushing, keep fighting, until the system that had oppressed them for so long was finally dismantled.

As Aisha walked home that night, she thought about the man in the coffee shop, about his warning to be careful. She knew he was right. They were stepping into dangerous territory now, challenging people who had the money and power to crush their movement if they weren't careful.

But Aisha wasn't afraid. She had come too far to back down now. The whispers in the shadows could no longer stay hidden. It was time to bring everything into the light.

Chapter 12: Loyalty and Betrayal

The more Aisha and her group uncovered about the hidden powers pulling the strings in the city, the more intense the pressure became. They had expected resistance from the outside—from the police, from the politicians, from the business leaders whose influence they were exposing—but what Aisha hadn't expected was the turmoil brewing within her own group. Loyalties were being tested, and it became increasingly clear that not everyone was as committed to the cause as they had seemed.

It all started with a small, seemingly innocent disagreement over strategy. After weeks of gathering evidence and preparing to go public with their findings, the group had begun debating how best to release the information. Some, like Aisha and Jason, wanted to hold a press conference and present the evidence directly to the public. Others felt it would be safer to leak the information anonymously through the media, fearing retaliation from the powerful forces they were challenging.

"I get that you want to be careful," Jason said during one of their meetings, his voice strained with frustration. "But hiding behind the media isn't going to get us the attention we need. We need to stand up and speak for ourselves, not let some reporters tell our story for us."

Emily, who had been quiet for most of the discussion, finally spoke up. "But we must think about the long-term consequences. If we put ourselves out there too much, we'll be putting targets on our backs. These people have money, connections—they'll come after us, and we won't be able to protect ourselves."

Aisha had heard this argument before, and while she understood the fear behind it, she couldn't shake the feeling that playing it safe wasn't the answer. "We've been playing it safe for too long," she said firmly. "And look where that's gotten us. If we're serious about exposing what's really going on, we must be willing to take risks."

The room was tense, divided between those who wanted to take bold action and those who were more cautious. It was a familiar tension, one that had surfaced in previous meetings, but now it seemed to be intensifying. Aisha could feel the cracks forming, and she wasn't sure how to bridge the divide.

After the meeting, Aisha stayed behind to talk with Jason. They were the last two left in the room, the hum of the city outside the only sound breaking the silence.

"Do you think they're right?" Aisha asked, her voice low. "That we're taking too many risks?"

Jason shook his head. "No. We've been careful, but we can't let fear stop us. If we don't go public with this, nothing's going to change. They'll just keep doing what they're doing, and no one will know."

Aisha nodded, but she couldn't shake the feeling that something was off. The disagreement about strategy was one thing, but there was something else—something she couldn't quite put her finger on. It wasn't until a few days later that her suspicions were confirmed.

It started with a leaked email. A local news outlet had somehow gotten hold of a private message between two members of their group, discussing the evidence they had gathered and their plans to release it. The leak wasn't devastating, but it was enough to alert their enemies that they were closing in, and suddenly, things started moving fast. The police union began issuing public statements defending their practices, local business leaders were giving interviews about the importance of "maintaining public safety," and the city council was scrambling to distance themselves from the controversy.

Someone in their group had betrayed them.

The realization hit Aisha like a punch to the gut. They had been so careful, so deliberate about keeping their plans within the group, but someone had broken that trust. Someone had handed their enemies the information they needed to prepare their defense before Aisha and her group could even go public.

Jason was furious when he found out. "I knew something like this would happen," he muttered, pacing back and forth in the small office they used for their meetings. "We've got a mole."

Aisha's mind raced as she tried to figure out who it could be. Everyone in the group had seemed so committed, so dedicated to the cause. But now, in light of the leak, she realized that she had been too trusting. The stakes were high, and it was possible that someone had been pressured or bribed into betraying them. It was also possible that fear had gotten the better of one of their members, and they had turned to protect themselves.

"We need to figure out who did this," Aisha said, her voice cold with anger. "Before they can do any more damage."

The group held an emergency meeting that night, but tensions were higher than ever. People were on edge, and the accusations flew almost immediately.

"It could've been anyone," one member said, throwing up his hands. "We've all been talking to the media, trying to get our message out. Maybe someone slipped up."

"I didn't slip up," Emily said defensively. "But I think we need to be realistic about what's happening here. Whoever leaked the email might have been trying to protect us from making a mistake."

Aisha shot Emily a sharp look. "Are you saying that betraying the group is somehow justified?"

"No, I'm just saying that maybe they were scared," Emily replied, her voice shaking. "We've all seen what happens to people who take on the system. People disappear, they lose their jobs, their reputations get ruined. Maybe someone thought they were doing the right thing."

Jason slammed his hand down on the table. "There's no 'right thing' about betrayal. Whoever did this put all of us in danger."

The room was silent, the weight of Jason's words sinking in. Aisha could feel the cracks widening, the fragile bonds of trust they had built over the past few months beginning to fray.

Over the next few days, the group's focus shifted from their original mission to figuring out who had betrayed them. The tension was palpable, and the more they dug, the more distrust began to spread. People who had once been allies now looked at each other with suspicion, and every conversation was laced with paranoia.

Aisha spent sleepless nights combing through emails, texts, and meeting notes, trying to find any clue that might point to the traitor. It was exhausting, and the longer it went on, the more she began to wonder if they would ever find out the truth.

Then, one evening, she got a call from Jason.

"I know who did it," he said, his voice tight with anger. "Meet me at the office."

Aisha's heart raced as she hurried to the office, her mind spinning with possibilities. When she arrived, Jason was already there, pacing back and forth in front of the desk. His face was pale, his jaw clenched.

"It was Emily," he said, his voice low but furious. "I found an email she sent to a council member's office, telling them what we were planning."

Aisha felt a wave of shock wash over her. Emily? She had always been cautious, sometimes too cautious, but Aisha had never thought she would betray the group. She had been there from the beginning, attending every meeting, marching in every protest. How could she do something like this?

"Why?" Aisha whispered, still trying to wrap her mind around the betrayal.

Jason shook his head. "I don't know. Fear, maybe. Or maybe they got to her—bribed her, threatened her. It doesn't matter why. What matters is that she sold us out."

The anger that had been simmering inside Aisha finally boiled over. She had trusted Emily, welcomed her into the group, listened to her ideas—even when they disagreed. And now, Emily had betrayed all of them, putting everything they had worked for at risk.

"What do we do now?" Aisha asked, her voice hard.

Jason looked at her, his eyes blazing. "We cut her out. She's done."

The next morning, Aisha called a meeting. When Emily arrived, she could sense that something was wrong. The room was colder, the faces around her more distant. And when Aisha confronted her with the email, Emily didn't deny it.

"I was trying to protect us," Emily said, tears welling up in her eyes. "I didn't want us to get hurt. You don't know what they're capable of. I thought—"

"You thought you could go behind our backs and betray everything we've been fighting for?" Aisha interrupted, her voice sharp. "You thought you could sell us out and call it protection?"

Emily's tears fell, but Aisha had no sympathy left. The betrayal was too deep.

"You're out," Jason said, his voice like steel. "We can't trust you anymore."

Emily left that day, and the group never saw her again. But the damage had been done. The betrayal had shaken them all, and it took weeks to rebuild the trust that had been shattered.

As Aisha sat alone in the office that night, she thought about loyalty and how fragile it could be. The fight for justice was not just about standing up to those in power—it was also about standing strong with those by your side. And not everyone had the strength to do that.

But Aisha did. And as long as she had Jason and the rest of her group, she knew they would keep fighting—no matter how many betrayals they faced.

Chapter 13: Cracks in the Armor

The betrayal had been a blow, but Aisha and her group refused to let it stop them. After Emily's departure, they tightened their circle, becoming more cautious about who they trusted and how they shared information. The tension was still there—an undercurrent of distrust that hadn't fully dissipated—but they knew they couldn't afford to lose focus. They had come too far, and the stakes were too high to give up now.

Despite the setbacks, there were signs that their efforts were starting to pay off. The pressure they had been applying to the city council, the police union, and the business leaders was beginning to expose cracks in the carefully constructed armor of those in power. The people who had always operated in the shadows were starting to feel the heat, and for the first time, Aisha could sense that they were on the defensive.

It started with a shift in public opinion. After the group's initial findings about the connections between business leaders, the police, and local politicians had been leaked to the media, more people began paying attention. News outlets that had previously ignored their movement were now covering the story, interviewing Aisha and Jason, and highlighting the systemic corruption that they had uncovered. What had once been dismissed as the grievances of a small, radical group was now becoming a broader conversation about justice and accountability.

The shift was slow at first, but it gained momentum with each passing week. People who had once been indifferent—or even hostile—toward their cause were starting to question the official narratives they had been fed. Community leaders began speaking out in support of Aisha's group, calling for more transparency in the city's decision-making process. Even a few local politicians, sensing the changing tide, cautiously voiced their concerns about the influence of money and power on the police force.

But the real turning point came when one of the city council members, a man named Councilman Rodriguez, reached out to Aisha directly. He had always been something of a wild card—never fully aligned with either side of the issue, but also never outspoken against the police or the business leaders. Aisha had assumed he would remain neutral, unwilling to take a stand one way or the other.

So, when she received an email from his office requesting a private meeting, she was both surprised and skeptical.

"I don't trust him," Jason said when Aisha told him about the request. "He's been sitting on the fence this whole time. Why would he suddenly want to talk to us?"

Aisha nodded, sharing Jason's doubts. But she also knew that if they were going to make real progress, they needed to start building alliances, even with people they didn't fully trust. "We should at least hear him out," she said. "If nothing else, it'll give us a sense of where he stands."

The meeting was arranged for the following week at a quiet café downtown, far from the usual political hotspots. When Aisha arrived, Councilman Rodriguez was already seated at a table in the back, a cup of coffee in front of him. He stood as she approached, offering a polite but guarded smile.

"Aisha, thanks for meeting with me," he said as they sat down.

Aisha nodded, watching him carefully. "I wasn't sure what to expect when I got your message. You've been pretty quiet on all this."

Rodriguez sighed, leaning back in his chair. "I know. I've been trying to figure out where I stand, to be honest. It's not easy being in the middle of something like this."

Aisha raised an eyebrow. "Middle? It seems pretty clear-cut to me. Either you support real accountability, or you're protecting the people who benefit from this system."

Rodriguez looked uncomfortable, his eyes darting around the café as if making sure no one was listening. "Look, I don't disagree with what you're fighting for. The police in this city have way too much unchecked power, and the connections between the union and the business community—it's problematic, to say the least. But you have to understand, there's a lot of pressure on us. These people... they have influence, and they know how to use it."

Aisha leaned forward, her voice calm but firm. "So, what are you saying? Are you here to tell me that you're too scared to do what's right?"

Rodriguez's face flushed, and for a moment, Aisha thought she had pushed too hard. But then he sighed again, this time with a sense of resignation. "No,

I'm here because I want to help. But I need to be smart about it. If I go up against these people head-on, I'll lose everything. They'll make sure of it."

Aisha felt a flicker of hope, but she kept her expression neutral. "What do you need from us?"

Rodriguez hesitated for a moment before speaking. "I've been in contact with a few other council members who feel the same way I do. They know things need to change, but they're afraid of the fallout. If you can keep the public pressure on—if you can keep exposing what's really going on—it'll give us the cover, we need to start pushing for real reforms."

Aisha's eyes narrowed. "And how do I know you won't turn on us when the heat gets too high?"

Rodriguez met her gaze, his expression serious. "You don't. But I'm not asking you to trust me blindly. I'm asking you to keep doing what you're doing, and if I can help make things move from the inside, I will."

It wasn't the full-throated support Aisha had hoped for, but it was something. She knew that politics was a game of leverage, and if Councilman Rodriguez could help them move the needle from within the system, it was worth pursuing.

"All right," Aisha said finally. "We'll keep the pressure on. But if you back down, if you leave us hanging, we'll come after you just like we've gone after everyone else."

Rodriguez nodded, a hint of respect in his eyes. "Fair enough."

The meeting ended on a cautious note, but as Aisha left the café, she felt a sense of momentum building. Councilman Rodriguez might not be the most reliable ally, but his willingness to engage was a sign that things were shifting. The cracks in the opposition's armor were starting to show.

Over the next few weeks, the group ramped up their efforts. They organized more protests, released more of their findings to the media, and continued to pressure the city council to take action. The more they pushed, the more public support they gained. People who had once dismissed them as radicals were now showing up to their protests, demanding change alongside them.

Even the police union, once untouchable, was starting to feel the strain. They held press conferences defending their practices, but their arguments rang hollow in the face of the mounting evidence. The more they tried to justify their actions, the more the public began to question why they had so much unchecked power in the first place.

Aisha could feel the tide turning. It wasn't a victory yet—far from it—but for the first time, it felt like they had a chance. The cracks in the system were widening, and the people in power were scrambling to hold it together.

But Aisha knew better than to let her guard down. The closer they got to real change, the more desperate their enemies would become. The fight was far from over, and she had no doubt that more challenges—and more betrayals—lay ahead.

Still, for the first time in a long time, Aisha allowed herself to hope. The cracks were there. And with enough pressure, the whole system might just come crashing down.

Chapter 14: The Cost of Silence

The deeper Aisha and her group delved into their fight for justice, the more she realized how much silence contributed to the very systems they were trying to dismantle. The cracks in the armor of the opposition were visible now, but they had only appeared because Aisha and her allies had refused to be silent. Yet so many other people with the power to speak out, people who knew what was going on—chose to remain silent. And that silence had a cost.

It was a conversation with her mother that brought this reality into sharp focus for Aisha. Her mother, who had always been supportive but cautious, had grown increasingly concerned about the risks Aisha was taking. She worried about the backlash, about the threats, about what might happen if Aisha pushed too far.

"I just don't want you to get hurt," her mother said one evening as they sat at the kitchen table. "I know you're doing the right thing, but there's so much at stake. These people don't play fair. They have power, and they'll use it."

Aisha had heard this argument before, not just from her mother, but from so many others—people who sympathized with the cause but who were too afraid to take a stand themselves. It was always the same fear: that speaking out, that challenging the system, would come with consequences they weren't prepared to face. But for Aisha, the consequences of staying silent were far worse.

"I get it, Mom," Aisha said, her voice steady but firm. "But if we don't speak out, if we don't fight back, then nothing will ever change. Silence is what they want. It's how they keep things the way they are."

Her mother sighed, her eyes filled with a mix of worry and pride. "I know. I just... I've seen what happens to people who challenge the system. It's not always fair. And I don't want to lose you."

Aisha reached across the table and took her mother's hand. "I'm not going anywhere. But I can't live with myself if I just sit back and let them keep doing this. You always taught me to stand up for what's right. That's what I'm doing."

Her mother nodded, her grip tightening on Aisha's hand. "I know. And I'm proud of you. I just worry."

Aisha understood her mother's fear, but it also made her think about all the people who, like her mother, had chosen to stay silent—not out of malice, but out of fear. That silence was what allowed the system to keep running, unchecked. It was what gave the people in power the freedom to continue exploiting, oppressing, and marginalizing communities like hers. Silence wasn't just inaction—it was complicity.

The next day, Aisha shared these thoughts with Jason as they prepared for their next protest. They were sitting in their usual spot at the community center, going over logistics and discussing the best way to keep the momentum going.

"It's the people who stay quiet that frustrate me the most," Aisha said, her voice tense. "I get why they're afraid, but their silence is what keeps the system in place. If more people spoke out, if more people refused to accept things the way they are, we could make real change."

Jason nodded, leaning back in his chair. "Yeah, I know what you mean. It's easy for people to stay quiet when it doesn't affect them directly. They can go on with their lives, pretend like nothing's wrong, and never have to face the consequences."

Aisha sighed, running her fingers through her hair. "And then there are the people who know exactly what's going on but still stay silent because it's easier for them. They don't want to risk their reputation, their jobs, their comfort."

Jason's expression darkened. "That's the worst. They benefit from the system, even if they don't say it out loud. They keep quiet because they're scared of losing what they have, even if it means watching others suffer."

It wasn't long before Aisha had a direct encounter with this kind of silence. A few days after her conversation with Jason, she received an invitation to speak at a panel on social justice at the local university. The event was being organized by a student group that had been inspired by her activism, and Aisha was excited about the opportunity to reach a new audience.

The panel itself went well—Aisha spoke passionately about the fight for police accountability, the need for systemic change, and the importance of standing up against injustice. The audience seemed engaged, nodding along with her points, and several students came up to her afterward to express their support.

But it was during the informal reception after the panel that Aisha had an unsettling conversation with one of the professors who had attended the event. He was an older man, with silver hair and a kind smile, the kind of person who seemed approachable and wise. He had come up to Aisha as she was grabbing a cup of coffee, introducing himself as Professor Hendricks.

"That was an impressive talk," he said, his voice warm. "You're doing important work."

"Thank you," Aisha replied, smiling. "I appreciate that."

The professor nodded, taking a sip of his coffee. "I've been following your movement closely. It's inspiring to see young people so engaged in the fight for justice."

Aisha felt a flicker of pride, but something about his tone made her cautious. There was a hint of hesitation, something unspoken lingering beneath his words.

"But?" Aisha asked, sensing there was more he wanted to say.

Professor Hendricks sighed, his expression growing more serious. "But I've been in this world for a long time, and I've seen movements like yours come and go. The system you're up against—it's bigger than you can imagine. It's deeply entrenched, and the people who control it aren't going to let go easily. I admire your courage, but I worry that you might be... setting yourself up for disappointment."

Aisha felt a wave of frustration rise within her. She had heard this before—this well-meaning warning that always seemed to come from people who weren't willing to take a stand themselves. People who claimed to understand the system but who remained silent, unwilling to risk their own comfort or security to challenge it.

"With all due respect, Professor," Aisha said, her voice steady but firm, "I'm not afraid of disappointment. I'm afraid of doing nothing. Silence is what lets them win."

The professor smiled, but there was a sadness in his eyes. "I'm not suggesting you do nothing, Aisha. I'm just saying that you have to be realistic about what you're up against. The people in power—they know how to wait things out. They've seen movements rise and fall, and they know that most people eventually give up."

Aisha bristled at his words, but she kept her tone measured. "I'm not most people."

The professor chuckled softly, shaking his head. "I hope you're right. But just be careful. The system has a way of wearing people down, even the most passionate activists."

As the professor walked away, Aisha felt a mix of anger and determination. She didn't need another warning about how hard the fight would be—she already knew that. What frustrated her was the professor's resignation, his quiet acceptance of a system that he knew was broken. He understood the injustice, but instead of speaking out, he chose to remain silent, watching from the sidelines as others took the risks, he wasn't willing to take.

That night, as Aisha lay in bed, she thought about all the people like Professor Hendricks—people who knew what was wrong but who stayed quiet, choosing to protect themselves rather than challenge the status quo. Their silence wasn't neutral—it was an active choice that allowed injustice to continue unchecked. And Aisha couldn't accept that.

The cost of silence, she realized, was not just the perpetuation of injustice. It was the erosion of hope, the slow grinding down of those who fought for change, leaving them isolated and vulnerable. Silence wasn't just inaction—it was a form of betrayal.

Aisha knew that she couldn't control the actions of others. She couldn't force people like Professor Hendricks to speak out or make her mother stop worrying about the risks. But she could refuse to be silent herself. She could keep fighting, keep pushing, keep speaking the truth, no matter how hard it got.

Because silence, in the face of injustice, was a cost she wasn't willing to pay.

Chapter 15: The Breaking Point

The momentum Aisha and her group had built was undeniable. More people were joining their protests, and the media coverage was growing. It felt like the movement was on the verge of something big—like real change was within reach. But as they gained ground, the opposition grew fiercer. The forces they were up against—business leaders, politicians, the police union—had been rattled, and now they were pushing back with everything they had.

The pressure was everywhere. The police had stepped up their presence at protests, and what had once been peaceful gatherings were now tense standoffs. Aisha had become a target. She noticed the way officers seemed to single her out, watching her more closely, their hands resting on their batons whenever she spoke to the crowd. Threatening letters started arriving at her door, anonymous notes telling her to stop what she was doing, warning her of what might happen if she didn't. The threats were never direct enough to go to the authorities, but they were unsettling all the same.

But Aisha wasn't afraid. Not yet. She had expected this. She knew the fight wouldn't be easy, and she wasn't going to back down. What she hadn't expected, though, was the strain the pressure would put on her group.

Tensions were rising, and the unity that had once held them together was beginning to fray. The betrayal they had uncovered a few weeks earlier had left a lingering sense of distrust. People were more cautious, more guarded with their words, afraid that another mole might be lurking among them. And now, with the full weight of the opposition bearing down on them, those cracks were starting to widen.

It began with small disagreements—about strategy, about how much risk they were willing to take, about whether they were pushing too hard, too fast. But the real breaking point came during one of their planning meetings, just a week before their biggest protest yet. They were organizing a march that would culminate at city hall, where they planned to confront the mayor and demand concrete action on police reform. The stakes were higher than ever, and everyone knew it.

As they sat around the table, going over the final details, the mood in the room was tense. Aisha could feel the weight of the moment pressing down on all of them.

"We need to make sure we're prepared for whatever they throw at us," Jason said, his voice steady but serious. "The police are going to be out in full force, and we can't let them intimidate us."

"Which is why we need to think about our safety," another member of the group, Malik, interjected. He had been one of the more cautious voices in the group, always pushing for a more measured approach. "I'm not saying we back down, but we need to be smart about this. If we push too hard, they'll use it as an excuse to crack down on us."

Aisha frowned, her frustration simmering beneath the surface. "We've been playing it safe for months and look where that's gotten us. If we don't make a strong stand now, we're going to lose all the momentum we've built."

Malik shook his head. "I'm not saying we play it safe. I'm saying we need to be strategic. We can't afford to get people hurt."

Jason jumped in; his voice more heated now. "People are already getting hurt, Malik. That's why we're out here in the first place. If we start pulling back now, they'll see it as a sign of weakness."

The argument escalated from there, voices growing louder as the group splintered into different camps. Some, like Jason, believed they needed to keep pushing, to show the city that they wouldn't be intimidated. Others, like Malik, were more concerned about the potential consequences, worried that the movement was growing too confrontational and that it could lead to violence.

Aisha sat in silence for a moment, watching the debate unfold, feeling the pressure building inside her. She understood both sides, but she couldn't shake the feeling that if they didn't go all in now, they might never get another chance. They were at a tipping point, and the way they handled this protest could determine the future of their entire movement.

Finally, Aisha stood up, cutting through the noise. "I get that we're all scared," she said, her voice calm but commanding. "I am too. But we've come too far to back down now. This march is about more than just us. It's about the people in this city who've been ignored, who've been oppressed, who've been told that their lives don't matter. If we don't make a stand now, when will we?"

The room fell silent as Aisha's words sank in. She could see the conflict in their faces, the fear mixed with determination. They all knew the risks. They had all seen what happened to movements like theirs when the pressure became too much. But they also knew that they couldn't afford to let fear stop them.

After a long pause, Jason nodded. "Aisha's right. We need to move forward. This isn't just about us—it's about the future."

Malik sighed, his expression tight with anxiety, but he didn't argue. "All right. But we need to make sure we're prepared. We need to have legal support on standby, and we need to make sure people know their rights."

The rest of the group murmured in agreement, and the tension in the room began to ease. They spent the next hour going over the final details, making sure everything was in place for the march. But as they wrapped up the meeting, Aisha couldn't shake the feeling that something had shifted. The unity that had once bound them together was fragile now, held together by a thin thread of shared purpose. And she knew that if anything went wrong at the march, that thread might snap.

The day of the march arrived with an almost unbearable weight of anticipation. The streets were packed with protesters, far more than Aisha had expected. It was a sea of people, all carrying signs, chanting for justice, demanding change. It was a beautiful sight, and for a moment, Aisha allowed herself to feel a sense of pride. They had built this. They had brought these people together.

But as the march moved toward city hall, the tension in the air became palpable. The police were out in full force, lining the streets, their presence a constant reminder of the threat that hung over the protest. Aisha could feel their eyes on her as she led the crowd, her heart pounding with a mixture of fear and determination.

They reached city hall without incident, but as the crowd gathered in front of the steps, Aisha noticed a group of officers moving closer, forming a line between the protesters and the building. The mayor was supposed to meet them, to hear their demands, but there was no sign of him. Instead, a police captain stepped forward, his expression hard.

"This is an illegal gathering," he announced, his voice amplified by a megaphone. "You need to disperse immediately, or you will be arrested."

A murmur of anger rippled through the crowd, but Aisha raised her hand, signaling for calm. This was what they had been waiting for—the moment when the system would try to silence them, to force them back into the shadows. But Aisha wasn't going to let that happen.

"We have a right to be here!" she shouted back; her voice strong despite the fear gnawing at her insides. "We have a right to demand justice!"

The crowd roared in agreement, and for a moment, Aisha thought they might be able to hold their ground. But then, without warning, the police moved in. The line of officers advanced, pushing through the crowd, grabbing protesters, dragging them to the ground. Chaos erupted, and Aisha felt herself swept up in the panic, her heart racing as she tried to keep the crowd from scattering.

But it was too late. The breaking point had come. The police were pushing back harder than they ever had before, and Aisha could see people being arrested, their arms twisted behind their backs, their faces pressed into the pavement. She tried to stay calm, to keep her focus, but the weight of it all—the fear, the anger, the overwhelming sense of betrayal—was too much.

And then, during the chaos, Aisha felt a hand grab her arm. She turned, expecting to see Jason or one of her friends, but instead, she found herself face-to-face with a police officer. His grip was tight, and before she could react, he shoved her to the ground, his knee pressing into her back as he pinned her down.

For a moment, everything went silent. The noise of the crowd, the shouts of the officers, the pounding of her heart—it all faded into the background. All Aisha could feel was the weight of the system pressing down on her, crushing her beneath its power.

But even as she lay there, her face pressed against the cold pavement, Aisha knew one thing: she wasn't broken. Not yet. And she wasn't going to stop fighting.

Because this was the breaking point—not for her, but for the system. And she was determined to see it fall.

Chapter 16: Rising From the Ashes

The aftermath of the protest was chaotic. The images of Aisha and her fellow protesters being arrested, thrown to the ground, and handcuffed had spread like wildfire across social media and the news. It was a moment of reckoning, not just for Aisha, but for the entire movement. As she sat in a holding cell at the local police station, her wrists sore from the tightness of the cuffs and her body aching from the force used against her, Aisha found herself teetering on the edge of exhaustion. But even in the cold, dimly lit cell, with the weight of the system pressing down on her, she refused to feel defeated.

They had pushed back hard, harder than she had expected. But their brutality only proved that the system was terrified of what Aisha and her group represented. The breaking point had come, and now it was time to rise from the ashes.

After a few hours, Aisha and the others were released. As she stepped out into the cool night air, she was met by Jason, Malik, and the rest of the group who had managed to avoid arrest. Their faces were tense, their bodies weary, but the fire in their eyes hadn't been extinguished.

"How are you feeling?" Jason asked as they walked away from the station, his voice low with concern.

Aisha rolled her shoulders, wincing at the pain that shot through her back. "I'm fine," she said, though the physical toll of the day had clearly worn her down. "We knew this could happen."

Jason nodded; his jaw clenched. "Yeah, but it doesn't make it any easier."

Malik, who had been quieter than usual, stepped up beside them. "The media's running with the story," he said, his voice heavy with both relief and uncertainty. "People are angry about what happened today. They're saying it was excessive force, that the police went too far."

Aisha allowed herself a small, grim smile. "Good. They should be angry. Maybe now people will start to see what we've been fighting against this whole time."

But even as she said the words, Aisha knew that anger alone wouldn't be enough. The protest had ended in violence, and the police had done exactly what she had feared—they had turned the narrative against them, painting the movement as dangerous and unruly. The images of police clashing with protest-ers were now being used to justify the crackdown, and Aisha knew that public opinion could be fickle.

The group reconvened at their usual meeting spot a few days later. The mood in the room was somber, the weight of what had happened at the protest still hanging over them. Some members of the group were shaken, their confi-dence rattled by the police response. Others were more determined than ever, their resolve hardening in the face of the crackdown.

Aisha stood at the front of the room, her eyes scanning the faces of the peo-ple who had become her closest allies. She could see the exhaustion in their eyes, the frustration, the fear. But she could also see something else: resilience. They hadn't come this far to give up now.

"We knew this fight wouldn't be easy," Aisha began, her voice steady despite the tension in the air. "What happened at the protest was hard, and I know some of you are feeling like we've hit a wall. But this is exactly what they want—to break us down, to make us doubt ourselves, to make us afraid. And we can't let them win."

There were murmurs of agreement, but Aisha could still feel the uncer-tainty lingering in the room. She knew they needed more than just a rallying cry—they needed a new plan.

"So, what do we do now?" Malik asked, his voice quiet but serious. "The police are cracking down harder than ever. If we keep pushing, things could get worse."

Aisha nodded. "We need to be smarter about how we move forward. The protest wasn't a failure, but it showed us that we need to adapt. We can't just rely on the streets—we need to attack the system on all fronts. That means legal action, community organizing, media campaigns. We need to make it clear that this isn't just about one protest. It's about changing the entire system."

Jason leaned forward, his eyes sharp with determination. "We've got lawyers who are willing to help us file lawsuits against the city for police bru-tality. We can use the footage from the protest to build a case. And we need to keep applying pressure on the city council. They've been quiet since the protest, but if we keep pushing, we can force them to take a stand."

Aisha nodded, feeling the energy in the room start to shift. They had been knocked down, but they weren't out. If anything, the brutality of the police response had given them even more reason to keep fighting. Now, they just had to be smarter about how they did it.

"We also need to take care of ourselves," Aisha added, her voice softer now. "This fight is long, and it's hard. We can't burn out. We need to support each other, make sure we're staying strong—physically, mentally, emotionally."

The group nodded in agreement, and for the first time since the protest, Aisha felt a sense of hope. They weren't going to let the system break them. They were going to rise from the ashes, stronger than before.

In the weeks that followed, Aisha and her group shifted their focus. They continued to organize protests, but they also started working on legal strategies to challenge the city and the police force. They held community meetings, bringing in lawyers and activists to educate people on their rights and how to protect themselves from police harassment. They built alliances with other social justice organizations, pooling their resources and expanding their reach.

The media attention they had garnered from the protest didn't fade. In fact, it intensified. News outlets were now regularly covering their movement, and Aisha found herself in the spotlight more than ever. She gave interviews, spoke at rallies, and used every platform she had to keep the pressure on the city.

And slowly, it started to work. The city council, which had been hesitant to engage with the movement before, began to feel the heat. Councilman Rodriguez, who had previously wavered in his support, publicly called for an independent investigation into the police response at the protest. Other council members, feeling the growing pressure from their constituents, started to express their support for police reform.

It wasn't a victory yet, but it was progress. The cracks in the system were widening, and Aisha knew that if they kept pushing, they could break through.

One evening, after a particularly long day of meetings and planning, Aisha sat alone in her apartment, reflecting on everything that had happened. The road ahead was still uncertain, and there were days when the weight of it all felt almost too heavy to bear. But as she thought about the people who had come together—people from all walks of life, united by a shared vision of justice—Aisha felt a renewed sense of purpose.

This was bigger than her. It was bigger than any one protest, any one battle. This was about changing the future, about making sure that the next generation didn't have to fight the same fight.

Aisha closed her eyes, letting the weight of the day fall away. She knew that the road ahead would be hard, and that the system would push back even harder. But she also knew that they had already come too far to turn back now.

They were rising from the ashes, and they weren't going to stop until the system was dismantled.

One afternoon, Aisha was sitting in the community center, preparing for a meeting with their legal team, when she received a message from an unfamiliar number. It was short and to the point:

"I'd like to meet with you. We have a common enemy. I believe I can help. —D."

Aisha stared at the message for a moment, her mind racing. The message was cryptic, and she didn't recognize the sender. But something about it piqued her curiosity. Whoever this person was, they seemed to know something important. Aisha had learned to be cautious, especially after the betrayal they had faced from within their group, but she also knew that they couldn't afford to ignore any potential allies—especially now.

She responded to the message cautiously, agreeing to meet at a public café in the city the following day.

When Aisha arrived at the café, she scanned the room, looking for anyone who seemed out of place. She had no idea who "D" was or what they wanted, but she was determined to find out. After a few minutes, a woman in her mid-40s, dressed in a sleek suit, approached her table. She had sharp eyes and an air of quiet confidence. Aisha had never seen her before, but something about her presence suggested she wasn't someone to be taken lightly.

"You're Aisha, right?" the woman asked, extending her hand. "I'm Danielle."

Aisha shook her hand, her curiosity growing. "You sent the message?"

Danielle nodded, sitting down across from Aisha. "I know this might seem strange, but I've been watching your movement closely. I believe we have some common goals."

Aisha raised an eyebrow. "And what would those be?"

Danielle leaned forward, her voice lowering. "I'm a lawyer. I've been working in corporate law for years, but recently I've been representing clients who've been impacted by the very system you're fighting against. Police misconduct, housing discrimination, labor rights violations—I've seen how deep the corruption runs. And I've seen how the people in power work to protect themselves at all costs."

Aisha listened carefully, unsure of where this was going. She had met lawyers before, but most of them were either hesitant to get involved or too focused on their careers to take risks.

"Why are you telling me this?" Aisha asked.

Danielle's expression softened, and for the first time, Aisha saw a hint of vulnerability in her eyes. "Because I've been part of that system for a long time. I've seen how it works from the inside, and I know how hard it is to fight against it. But I'm tired of watching people suffer while the rich and powerful stay untouchable. I want to help."

Aisha was silent for a moment, processing Danielle's words. It wasn't often that someone from the corporate world reached out to offer support. But Aisha also knew that sometimes the most valuable allies came from unexpected places.

"What kind of help are you offering?" Aisha asked, her voice cautious but curious.

Danielle leaned back in her chair, her sharp eyes scanning the café as if to make sure no one was listening. "I have access to information—financial records, contracts, communications between politicians and business leaders. I can get you documents that prove the corruption you're up against. But more importantly, I can help you navigate the legal system in ways that will make an impact."

Aisha's heart raced at the possibilities. Having someone with Danielle's experience on their side could be a game-changer. But she still wasn't sure why Danielle had chosen to approach them now.

"Why us?" Aisha asked, her voice tinged with skepticism. "You could go public with this information on your own."

Danielle smiled, but there was a hint of sadness behind it. "I've spent years working in the system. I know how it works. Going public on my own wouldn't do much. The media would spin it, the people in power would cover it up, and I'd be dismissed as just another disgruntled lawyer. But your movement has momentum. People are listening to you. If we work together, we can make sure the truth gets out—and that it's impossible for them to ignore."

Aisha considered Danielle's offer carefully. She knew that working with someone like Danielle came with risks. There was always the possibility that she had her own agenda or that her involvement could complicate things. But Aisha also knew that if Danielle was telling the truth, the information she had could be exactly what they needed to break through the wall of corruption that was protecting the people in power.

After a long pause, Aisha nodded. "Okay. Let's see what we can do together."

Over the next few weeks, Danielle became an invaluable asset to the movement. She provided Aisha's group with documents that proved the financial ties between the police union, local business leaders, and city politicians. She helped them craft legal strategies that would force the city to confront the corruption head-on. And most importantly, she brought a new level of credibility to their fight.

With Danielle's help, Aisha and her group began to file lawsuits against the city for police misconduct and civil rights violations. They held press conferences, armed with the documents Danielle had provided, showing the public the undeniable connections between the police, the business community, and the politicians who were benefiting from the status quo. The media couldn't ignore the story now, and public outrage grew.

But as the movement gained strength, Aisha noticed something else: they were starting to attract more allies, not just from the corporate world, but from within the political system itself. Councilman Rodriguez had been their first cautious ally, but now, other politicians were quietly reaching out, offering their support. Some were doing it because they believed in the cause, while others were simply trying to protect their own reputations as the tide of public opinion shifted. Either way, Aisha knew that these alliances could help push the movement forward.

One evening, as Aisha and Jason sat in the community center, going over their latest strategy, Jason leaned back in his chair, a small smile on his face.

"I never thought we'd be working with lawyers and politicians," he said, shaking his head. "But here we are."

Aisha smiled, though her mind was still racing with everything that had happened over the past few weeks. "Yeah, it's strange. But sometimes you must work with the system to break it down."

Jason nodded, his expression growing more serious. "Do you trust Danielle?"

Aisha paused, considering the question. "I don't know if I trust her completely. But I think she's sincere about wanting to help. And for now, we need her."

Jason leaned forward, resting his elbows on the table. "I just hope we're not getting in too deep. These alliances are powerful, but they come with risks. We've got to make sure we don't lose sight of what we're fighting for."

Aisha nodded, understanding Jason's concern. It was easy to get caught up in the power plays, the legal strategies, and the media attention. But at the core of their movement was a simple truth: they were fighting for justice, for the people in their community who had been ignored and oppressed for too long.

As Aisha looked around the room, at the faces of her friends and allies, she felt a renewed sense of purpose. The fight wasn't over—not by a long shot. But for the first time in a long time, it felt like they had the tools and the support they needed to take on the system in a way that could make a difference.

They had allies now—unexpected allies—but Aisha knew that they couldn't rely on anyone else to win this fight for them. The power still lay in the hands of the people, and it was up to them to keep pushing, to keep fighting, until the system finally came crashing down.

Chapter 18: The Price of Progress

As Aisha's movement gained momentum, the victories began to pile up. Lawsuits against the city were making headlines, and the documents Danielle had provided were shaking the political establishment to its core. The public outrage was growing, and people were no longer willing to accept the corruption and violence that had been simmering under the surface for so long. It felt like they were on the verge of something transformative—a moment when real change could happen.

But with every victory came a new challenge. The opposition wasn't retreating; they were digging in, fighting back harder than ever. The police union had ramped up their defense, launching a public relations campaign to paint the protesters as dangerous radicals who were destabilizing the city. Business leaders were holding closed-door meetings with politicians, trying to find ways to quash the movement without sparking even more public outrage. The stakes were higher than ever, and Aisha could feel the pressure building from all sides.

One evening, after a particularly grueling day of meetings and legal planning, Aisha found herself sitting in her apartment, staring at her phone. The screen was filled with messages—supporters offering encouragement, journalists asking for interviews, lawyers updating her on the latest developments. But mixed in with those were the threats. They came in waves now—emails, social media comments, even letters slipped under her door. The tone was always the same: stop what you're doing, or you'll regret it.

Aisha had always known that standing up to the system would come with risks. But now, those risks were becoming more real, more personal. She had been followed on the streets more than once, strange cars idling outside her apartment at odd hours. She could see the weariness in Jason's face, the tension in Malik's voice, as the toll of the fight began to weigh on all of them. They had been prepared for backlash, but the level of intimidation they were facing was beyond anything they had anticipated.

It wasn't just the external threats that were wearing on Aisha. The internal dynamics of the movement were becoming more complicated as well. As the group grew larger and more successful, they attracted new members—some of whom had their own ideas about how the movement should be run. Disagreements over strategy, tactics, and messaging were becoming more frequent, and Aisha found herself spending more time managing conflicts within the group than focusing on their broader goals.

One night, after a particularly heated meeting where members had argued over the direction of the movement, Aisha sat alone in the community center, her head in her hands. The pressure was getting to her, and she couldn't shake the feeling that the movement was starting to fracture. They had always prided themselves on being a unified front, but now, with so many voices and so many agendas, it felt like they were losing their way.

Jason found her there, sitting in the dark. He didn't say anything at first, just pulled up a chair beside her and sat in silence.

"I'm worried," Aisha said finally, her voice barely above a whisper. "I feel like we're losing control. The more progress we make, the more it feels like we're falling apart."

Jason nodded; his face etched with concern. "Yeah, I've noticed it too. The pressure's getting to everyone. It's hard to keep people focused when we're being pulled in so many directions."

Aisha sighed, leaning back in her chair. "I knew this was going to be hard. But I didn't expect it to feel so... heavy. Like every decision we make could either push us forward or completely unravel everything."

Jason leaned forward, resting his elbows on his knees. "That's the price of progress, right? The more ground we gain, the harder they push back. And the more people we bring in, the harder it is to keep everyone on the same page."

Aisha nodded, but the weight of it all still pressed down on her. "I just don't want us to lose sight of what we're fighting for. The bigger we get, the more complicated it becomes, and I don't want to wake up one day and realize we've become the very thing we're fighting against."

Jason was quiet for a moment before he spoke. "We won't let that happen. We just need to refocus. We've always been good at adapting, at finding new ways to push forward. We can do it again."

Aisha knew Jason was right, but she also knew that the challenges they were facing now were different from anything they had dealt with before. The stakes were higher, the opposition more determined, and the fractures within their own group were becoming harder to ignore.

The next day, Aisha called a meeting with the core members of the movement—Jason, Malik, Danielle, and a few others who had been with them from the beginning. They sat around the table, the tension in the room palpable. Aisha knew they needed to have a difficult conversation, but it was one that couldn't be avoided any longer.

"We've been doing a lot of good work," Aisha began, her voice calm but firm. "We've made progress that I didn't think was possible when we first started. But we're also facing some real challenges—both from the outside and from within. If we're going to keep moving forward, we need to address those challenges head-on."

The group nodded, their faces serious. They all knew what Aisha was talking about—the internal conflicts, the growing number of voices pulling the movement in different directions, the pressure of managing their newfound success.

"We need to get back to our core principles," Aisha continued. "We started this movement with a clear goal: to fight for justice, to dismantle the systems that are oppressing our communities. But lately, it feels like we're losing sight of that. We're getting caught up in the politics, in the media attention, in the legal battles. Those things are important, but they can't be the only focus. We need to remember why we're doing this in the first place."

Malik nodded, his voice thoughtful. "We've been stretched thin. We're trying to fight on so many fronts, and it's pulling us apart. Maybe we need to prioritize—focus on the areas where we can make the biggest impact, rather than trying to take on everything at once."

Danielle, who had been quiet until now, spoke up. "I agree. The legal battles are important, but we can't let them consume all our energy. We need to keep the community engaged, keep the grassroots movement alive. That's where our strength comes from."

Jason leaned forward; his eyes intense. "We also need to make sure we're taking care of each other. This fight is long, and it's brutal. We've all been feeling the strain, and if we don't support each other, we're going to burn out."

Aisha nodded, grateful for the honesty in the room. These were the people she trusted most, the ones who had been with her through the toughest parts of the fight. She knew they could get through this, but it was going to require some difficult decisions.

Over the next few days, the group worked to streamline their efforts. They refocused on their core goals, deciding to prioritize community organizing and public outreach, while keeping the legal battles in motion. They also implemented a system of rotating leadership, allowing different members of the group to take on responsibilities and give others a chance to rest and recharge.

The changes weren't easy, and there were still disagreements and tensions to navigate. But slowly, the sense of unity that had once defined the movement began to return. Aisha could feel the shift. They were moving forward again—not just as a loose coalition of activists, but as a focused, determined force for change.

But even as they regrouped, Aisha knew the hardest part was still ahead. The system they were fighting wasn't going to go down without a fight. The police, the business leaders, the politicians—they had too much at stake to let the movement succeed without a struggle. And as the movement gained more ground, the backlash would only intensify.

A few weeks after their strategic meeting, Aisha received a call from Danielle. Her voice was urgent, and Aisha could hear the tension in her words.

"I just got some disturbing news," Danielle said. "There's a private meeting happening tonight between some of the city's biggest business leaders and a few high-ranking police officials. They're planning something—something big."

Aisha's heart raced. "What do you mean?"

"I don't have all the details yet," Danielle replied. "But from what I've heard, they're looking for ways to shut us down for good. They're worried that we're getting too close, that we're gaining too much power. They're scared—and they're going to do whatever it takes to stop us."

Aisha felt a chill run down her spine. She had known from the beginning that they were taking on powerful forces, but hearing it laid out like this made the threat feel even more real.

"What do we do?" Aisha asked, her voice steady despite the fear gnawing at her insides.

"We need to be prepared," Danielle said. "They're going to come after us hard, and we need to make sure we're ready. This is going to get ugly."

Aisha hung up the phone, her mind racing. The price of progress was becoming clear. The more they pushed, the harder the system pushed back. But Aisha wasn't going to back down. She couldn't. The fight was too important.

As she gathered her thoughts and prepared to meet with her group, Aisha knew one thing for certain: they were in this for the long haul, and no matter what the opposition threw at them, they weren't going to stop.

Because this wasn't just about winning a battle. It was about changing the future. And Aisha was willing to pay whatever price that took.

Chapter 19: A Storm Brewing

Aisha couldn't shake the unease that had settled in her chest after Danielle's phone call. The idea of the city's most powerful business leaders and high-ranking police officials meeting in secret to plot against their movement wasn't surprising—it was a tactic she had expected from the beginning. But now, with their recent progress threatening the status quo, the sense of impending danger had become more tangible. The storm was brewing, and Aisha knew they needed to prepare for the worst.

The next day, Aisha gathered her core team—Jason, Malik, Danielle, and a few of their most trusted allies—to discuss the situation. They met at the community center, their usual safe space for planning and organizing. But today, the room felt different, heavier, as if the weight of the entire city was pressing down on them.

"We're in the crosshairs," Aisha began, her voice steady but filled with urgency. "Danielle got word of a secret meeting between business leaders and the police. They're planning something big—something to take us down. We don't know the specifics yet, but we need to assume they're going to escalate their efforts to shut us down."

Jason leaned forward; his jaw clenched. "It was only a matter of time before they started pulling out all the stops. We've been hitting them hard, and they're not going to just sit back and let us win."

Danielle nodded, her face tense with concern. "I've been trying to gather more information, but these meetings are happening behind closed doors, and they're being very careful about who knows what. What I do know is that they're worried. Our lawsuits are gaining traction, and public opinion is shifting in our favor. They're feeling threatened, and that makes them dangerous."

Malik frowned; his arms crossed over his chest. "So, what do we do? We can't back down, but we also can't afford to be reckless. If they're planning to come after us, we need to be smart."

Aisha nodded, agreeing with Malik's caution. "We're not going to back down, but we do need to be prepared. First, we need to make sure our legal team is ready to respond to any retaliation. We've already seen how they're trying to smear us in the media, and it's only going to get worse. We need to protect ourselves legally, and we need to make sure the public knows the truth."

Jason spoke up, his voice firm. "We also need to keep the pressure on. If they're planning something, we need to hit them before they have a chance to strike. We should organize another protest, something big enough to keep the momentum going and show them that we're not afraid."

Aisha hesitated for a moment. The idea of organizing another large-scale protest so soon after the last one—where they had faced police violence, and several members of the group had been arrested—made her uneasy. She knew they couldn't afford to lose their momentum, but she also knew that pushing too hard, too fast could backfire.

"We'll organize another protest," Aisha said finally, her voice calm. "But this time, we need to be even more strategic. We need to anticipate their moves and be ready for anything. This isn't just about making noise—it's about making sure we come out on top."

Danielle nodded in agreement. "I can reach out to some of my contacts in the media. We'll need to make sure that whatever happens, the story is told from our perspective. If the police escalate again, we need the world to see it."

The group spent the rest of the afternoon strategizing, going over every detail of the upcoming protest and discussing ways to protect themselves legally and publicly. Aisha felt a sense of determination rising within her, but the nagging fear of what might happen next lingered in the back of her mind. They were walking a fine line, and one wrong move could unravel everything they had worked for.

As the days passed, Aisha and her team kept a close eye on the city's leaders, looking for any sign of what they might be planning. Tensions were rising across the city, and it wasn't just the movement that was feeling the strain. The business community was increasingly vocal about the impact the protests were having on their operations, while the police force seemed to be growing more aggressive in their tactics. Something was coming. Aisha could feel it.

One evening, just days before their planned protest, Danielle called Aisha with new information. Her voice was tight with urgency.

"They're planning a raid," Danielle said, her words tumbling out quickly. "I don't know all the details yet, but I've heard whispers that the police are going to raid one of our organizing spaces. They're looking for an excuse to shut us down, and they're hoping to find something—anything—that will justify their actions."

Aisha's stomach dropped. A raid could be devastating, not just because of the legal implications, but because it would give the police the narrative, they needed to paint the movement dangerous and criminal.

"We need to move everything," Aisha said, her mind already racing through their next steps. "Anything they could use against us—documents, equipment, supplies—it needs to be out of our organizing spaces before they make their move."

Danielle agreed. "I'll help you coordinate. But we need to be quick. They could act any day now."

Aisha immediately called Jason and Malik, and together, they began the process of clearing out their main organizing spaces. They moved their most sensitive materials to safer locations, relying on trusted allies to store them. It was a tense, sleepless few days as they prepared for the worst, unsure of when or where the police would strike.

The raid came early one morning, just hours after they had finished relocating their supplies. Aisha received a frantic call from one of their volunteers, who had been outside the community center when the police arrived in force, swarming the building with a show of power that was clearly meant to intimidate.

"They're everywhere," the volunteer said, her voice shaking. "They've blocked off the entire block. They're going through everything."

Aisha's heart pounded in her chest, but she forced herself to stay calm. "Don't panic. We've moved everything important. They're not going to find anything."

The raid lasted for hours, with police officers tearing through the community center, searching for anything that could be used against the movement. But thanks to their quick action, they found nothing. By the time the media arrived, it was clear that the police had overplayed their hand. The raid, which was meant to discredit the movement, ended up backfiring spectacularly.

The news coverage painted the raid as an unnecessary show of force, and public opinion shifted even further in Aisha's favor. People were outraged that the police had targeted a peaceful movement, and the city's leaders found themselves on the defensive.

In the days that followed, Aisha and her team capitalized on the public outrage, organizing press conferences, giving interviews, and rallying more support for their cause. The raid, which had been meant to silence them, had only made them louder.

But even as they celebrated this victory, Aisha knew that the storm was far from over. The raid had been a warning shot, a signal that the people in power were willing to go to extreme lengths to protect their interests. The next time, they wouldn't just be trying to intimidate—they'd be trying to destroy.

Aisha gathered her team together after the raid, and as they sat around the table, she looked at each of them, her expression serious.

"We won this round," Aisha said, her voice steady. "But we can't let our guard down. They're going to come at us harder next time. We need to be ready."

Jason nodded, his face tense but determined. "They're scared. That means we're getting close. But we need to be smart about how we move forward."

Malik leaned forward, his voice low. "What's the next move?"

Aisha took a deep breath. "We keep going. We keep organizing, we keep filing lawsuits, we keep applying pressure. But we also need to build stronger alliances. We can't do this alone."

Danielle nodded in agreement. "I've already reached out to a few other organizations. They're willing to help, but we need to be careful. The more powerful we become, the more dangerous we are to them."

Aisha looked around the room, at the faces of the people who had become her family in this fight. The storm was coming, and they all knew it. But they weren't going to back down.

"We've come too far to stop now," Aisha said, her voice filled with determination. "Let them try to tear us down. We'll rise stronger every time."

Chapter 20: Strength in Numbers

The raid had been a wake-up call for Aisha and her team. It showed them just how far the system was willing to go to protect itself, but it also revealed something else: they were becoming too powerful to ignore. Public support was growing, and with every failed attempt to silence them, the city's leaders were only strengthening the movement they were trying to destroy.

But Aisha knew they couldn't rely solely on the public outrage from the raid. The storm was still brewing, and the people in power weren't going to stop. If they wanted to survive the coming battles, they needed to expand their reach and build stronger alliances. It was no longer just about protesting in the streets or filing lawsuits. It was about creating a network of allies that could help them withstand whatever came next.

In the weeks following the raid, Aisha threw herself into the work of coalition-building. She reached out to other social justice organizations—groups that had been fighting similar battles in other parts of the city, and even across the country. She connected with labor unions, housing advocates, environmental justice groups, and civil rights organizations. The goal was to create a broad-based movement that could not only withstand the pressure from the authorities but also push for systemic change on multiple fronts.

One of the first groups to join forces with Aisha's movement was a local labor union that had been fighting for workers' rights in the city's underfunded public services. The union had been battling low wages, unsafe working conditions, and the privatization of public services for years, and they saw Aisha's fight against police brutality and corruption as part of the same struggle.

"Your fight is our fight," said Denise, the head of the union, during their first meeting. She was a tough, no-nonsense woman who had been organizing workers for decades. "They're trying to keep us divided, to make us believe that our issues are separate. But they're all connected. The same people who are underfunding our schools, cutting our wages, and trying to privatize everything are the ones protecting the police and keeping the status quo. We need to come together."

Aisha nodded, grateful for Denise's insight and leadership. "We've been saying that from the beginning—that the system is built to oppress us in every way. If we want real change, we need to take on the whole system, not just one piece of it."

Over the next few weeks, Aisha and Denise worked together to organize joint actions—protests, community meetings, and public forums that brought together workers, activists, and community members from different backgrounds. The response was overwhelming. People who had previously felt isolated in their struggles began to see the connections between their issues and the broader fight for justice. The movement was growing, and with it, the sense of collective power.

But as the movement expanded, Aisha also began to realize that their growing power came with new challenges. The more people they brought into the fold, the more difficult it became to keep everyone on the same page. Different groups had different priorities, different ways of organizing, and different approaches to the fight. While they all shared the same overall goal—dismantling the oppressive systems that kept them down—they didn't always agree on the best way to get there.

One afternoon, Aisha found herself in a heated discussion with some of the newer members of the coalition. They were younger, more radical in their approach, and they believed that the movement needed to adopt more confrontational tactics—direct action, civil disobedience, and even property damage—if they wanted to send a message to those in power.

"We've tried peaceful protests, and what did that get us?" said Marcus, a passionate young activist who had recently joined the movement. "They raided our spaces, arrested our people, and tried to crush us. If we want to show them, we're serious, we need to hit them where it hurts."

Aisha listened carefully, understanding where Marcus was coming from. She, too, had felt the rage boiling inside her after the raid, the desire to strike back at the system that had oppressed her and her community for so long. But she also knew that escalating the conflict in that way could alienate some of their supporters and give the police the justification they were looking for to crack down even harder.

"I get it," Aisha said, her voice calm but firm. "I'm angry too. But we need to be smart about how we move forward. If we escalate too quickly, we risk losing the public support we've worked so hard to build. And that's exactly what they want. They want us to give them an excuse to label us as violent, to turn the media and the public against us."

Marcus frowned, clearly frustrated. "So, what are we supposed to do? Just keep playing by their rules, waiting for them to crush us?"

"No," Aisha said, meeting his gaze. "We don't play by their rules. But we also don't let them dictate how we fight. We need to be strategic, to use every tool we have—protests, legal action, media campaigns, coalition-building. We're not just fighting for ourselves; we're fighting for everyone who's been left behind by this system. We need to keep the bigger picture in mind."

The room was silent for a moment as Marcus considered her words. Aisha could see the conflict in his eyes—the tension between the desire for immediate action and the need for long-term strategy. She understood that tension because she felt it herself every day. But as the leader of this movement, it was her job to keep them focused, to make sure they didn't lose sight of what they were fighting for.

Eventually, Marcus nodded, though he still looked unsatisfied. "I hear you. I just hope we don't lose the fire."

"We won't," Aisha said, her voice steady. "We'll keep the fire, but we'll use it wisely."

As the weeks went on, Aisha and her coalition continued to grow. They brought in environmental justice groups who were fighting for clean air and water in the city's poorest neighborhoods, where pollution was rampant. They connected with housing advocates who were battling gentrification and displacement, fighting to keep families in their homes. They built relationships with immigrant rights organizations that were challenging the city's harsh immigration enforcement policies.

Each new group brought its own perspective, its own expertise, and its own set of priorities. And while it wasn't always easy to navigate the competing interests and approaches, Aisha knew that their strength lay in their diversity. The more people they brought into the movement, the harder it would be for the system to ignore them.

But with that growth came new risks. The authorities weren't blind to what was happening, and they were watching Aisha's every move. The police had stepped up their surveillance, monitoring their protests, tapping into their communications, and trying to find ways to undermine their efforts. Aisha knew they were being watched, but she refused to let it deter her.

"We knew this wasn't going to be easy," she said one evening as she and Jason sat in the community center, reviewing their plans for an upcoming rally. "But we've got something they can't take from us: the people. As long as we keep building, as long as we stay focused on the people we're fighting for, we're going to win."

Jason nodded; his eyes filled with determination. "You're right. But we've also got to be careful. The bigger we get, the more they're going to try to tear us apart."

Aisha sighed, knowing that Jason was right. The more powerful they became, the more vulnerable they were to attacks from the inside and the outside. It was a delicate balance, one that required constant vigilance.

But Aisha wasn't afraid of the challenge. She had always known that this fight would be long and difficult. And now, with the strength of a broad coalition behind her, she felt more confident than ever that they could win.

As the movement grew and their network of allies expanded, Aisha could feel the tide turning. The storm that had been brewing for so long was about to break. And when it did, she knew they would be ready.

Chapter 21: Eyes on the Horizon

As the coalition continued to grow, Aisha could feel the winds of change sweeping through the city. It wasn't just the protests or the lawsuits that were making a difference—people were beginning to believe that real change was possible. Neighborhoods that had once been ignored were now at the center of a citywide conversation about justice, equity, and accountability. The movement Aisha had started with a few close friends had blossomed into something bigger than any of them had ever imagined.

But with the taste of progress came a sense of heightened responsibility. Aisha had never sought out the spotlight, but now, as the de facto leader of the movement, she found herself the focal point of attention, both from supporters and from those who wanted to see her fail. The media was constantly requesting interviews, and more and more, her face was becoming synonymous with the fight for justice in the city.

One morning, as Aisha was sitting in her apartment, trying to catch a rare moment of quiet, she received a call from a city official. It was unexpected—city officials rarely reached out to her unless they were responding to one of the lawsuits or protests. But this call was different. The official, a senior advisor to the mayor, wanted to meet.

"They're ready to talk," the advisor had said over the phone, his voice measured. "I think they're starting to realize that ignoring you isn't working. The mayor wants to have a conversation about reforms."

Aisha had felt a rush of adrenaline at those words. For months, the mayor had been stonewalling their demands, refusing to engage in any meaningful dialogue about police reform or systemic change. But now, with the pressure mounting and public opinion shifting, it seemed that the city's leadership was finally willing to come to the table.

But as exciting as the prospect of negotiations was, Aisha also felt a gnawing sense of caution. She knew that these conversations, if they happened, would be fraught with compromises and political maneuvering. The city wasn't going to hand over reforms without a fight, and Aisha didn't want to be used as a symbol of progress without seeing real change take place.

She called a meeting with her core team—Jason, Malik, Danielle, and Denise—to discuss the possibility of sitting down with the mayor. They met at the community center, their usual base of operations, where the walls were now covered with posters, news clippings, and signs from their protests.

"The mayor's team reached out," Aisha said, getting straight to the point. "They want to meet. Apparently, they're ready to talk about reforms."

Jason raised an eyebrow, his expression skeptical. "Ready to talk or ready to make a deal that makes them look good without actually changing anything?"

Aisha nodded. "That's what I'm worried about too. We've seen this before, leaders who talk about a big game about reform but don't do anything meaningful. But if we don't at least hear them out, we could miss an opportunity to push for real change."

Malik leaned forward; his face serious. "We must be careful. This could be a trap. They might try to divide us—offer just enough to satisfy some of our demands but not enough to make a real difference. We can't let them co-opt the movement."

Danielle, always the strategist, chimed in. "The fact that they want to meet at all is a sign that they're feeling the pressure. We have leverage right now, but we need to make sure we use it wisely. If we go into those talks, we need to be clear about what we're demanding, and we can't accept anything less than real, concrete commitments."

Aisha listened carefully to each of them, her mind racing with the possibilities. She knew they had to be strategic, but she also didn't want to pass up an opportunity to finally see some of their demands met. The movement had been pushing for months, and this could be the moment when their efforts finally paid off.

"We need to be united going into this," Aisha said after a moment. "If we're going to sit down with the mayor, we need to be clear about our non-negotiables. We can't let them offer us cosmetic changes and call it reform."

The group nodded in agreement, and over the next hour, they outlined their demands: meaningful police reform, including changes to use-of-force policies and the creation of an independent oversight board; investments in communities that had been neglected for too long; and an end to the city's discriminatory practices in housing and education. These were the issues they had been fighting for from the beginning, and Aisha was determined not to walk away from the talks without real commitments.

A few days later, Aisha and her team met with the mayor and his advisors at city hall. The atmosphere was tense from the start. The mayor, a seasoned politician, greeted them with a smile, but Aisha could sense the caution in his eyes. He knew the power they held now—power that had been earned through months of protests, legal battles, and coalition-building.

"Thank you for coming," the mayor said as they sat down at a long conference table. "I want to start by saying that I recognize the importance of the work you've been doing. The city is listening, and we're ready to make changes."

Aisha nodded, keeping her expression neutral. "We appreciate that, but we're here because we need to see real action. We've outlined our demands, and we're not interested in half measures."

The mayor's smile tightened slightly, but he nodded. "Of course. We've reviewed your demands, and we're willing to make some commitments. We're prepared to allocate additional funding to community programs, and we're open to revisiting the police department's use-of-force policies."

Aisha listened carefully, but her instincts told her this was only the surface. She glanced at Danielle, who gave a subtle nod, signaling that the concessions weren't enough.

"That's a start," Aisha said, her voice measured. "But we're not here for symbolic gestures. We need a commitment to independent oversight of the police department, with real power to investigate misconduct and hold officers accountable. And we need significant investments in housing, education, and healthcare for our communities. Without that, there's no point in continuing this conversation."

The mayor's advisors shifted uncomfortably in their seats, and for a moment, Aisha thought the meeting might fall apart. But then the mayor leaned forward, his expression serious.

"We understand your position," he said slowly. "And we're willing to discuss those issues further. But we need to make sure any changes we implement are sustainable and don't destabilize the city."

Aisha felt a surge of frustration at the mayor's careful words. She had heard this argument before—the idea that pushing for too much change too quickly would somehow lead to chaos. But she knew that was just a way of protecting the status quo.

"That's exactly what they always say," Jason said, his voice hard. "They want us to believe that incremental change is the only option because they're scared of losing control."

The mayor's eyes flicked to Jason, but Aisha cut in before the conversation could derail. "We're not asking for anything radical. We're asking for justice. And justice means making real, meaningful changes to a system that's been broken for a long time."

The room fell silent for a moment, the weight of Aisha's words hanging in the air. She could see the mayor and his advisors' exchanging glances, calculating their next move. This was the moment of truth—where they would either agree to real change or continue the cycle of empty promises.

Finally, the mayor spoke. "We're willing to commit to an independent oversight board for the police, with subpoena power and the authority to investigate misconduct. And we're prepared to work with your coalition to invest in community-based programs. But we need time to implement these changes."

Aisha nodded slowly. It wasn't everything they wanted, but it was a significant step forward—one that could lay the groundwork for even more progress in the future.

"We'll hold you to that," Aisha said, her voice firm. "And we'll keep pushing until we see the changes happen."

The meeting ended with a tentative agreement. The mayor's office would announce the creation of the independent oversight board and commit to investing in community programs. It wasn't the end of the fight, but it was the beginning of a new phase—one where the movement's influence was undeniable, and the city's leadership had no choice but to engage.

As Aisha and her team left city hall, she felt a mixture of relief and caution. They had won a significant victory, but she knew the real work was just beginning. They would have to stay vigilant, to ensure that the promises made in that room were kept.

Later that evening, as Aisha stood on the steps of the community center, looking out at the city that had become the battleground for their movement, she felt a sense of both pride and responsibility. The horizon was still far away, and the road ahead would be filled with challenges. But for the first time, she could see the possibility of real change, not just for her community, but for the entire city.

They had come this far together, and Aisha knew they would keep going eyes on the horizon, ready to face whatever came next.

Chapter 22: Holding the Line

After the meeting with the mayor, the city's commitment to police reform and community investment made headlines. The announcement of an independent oversight board with real investigative power was hailed as a victory, not just for Aisha's movement but for everyone who had been fighting against systemic injustice for years. But for Aisha, the victory felt fragile, like a promise written in the sand—easy to wash away if they didn't stay vigilant.

The next few weeks were a whirlwind. The media attention was relentless, with reporters constantly seeking Aisha out for interviews, asking her how she felt about the city's promises. Aisha knew the importance of managing the narrative—of keeping the public's focus on the need for accountability. But she also knew that the real battle was just beginning. Making promises in front of cameras was one thing; following through with concrete actions was another.

"We can't let up," Aisha told her core team one afternoon as they sat in the community center, reviewing the mayor's public statements. "This oversight board is a step in the right direction, but we all know how these things go. If we're not watching them every step of the way, they'll water it down until it's meaningless."

Jason nodded, his expression serious. "They're already trying to spin it like it's a huge win for them. Like they've done us some kind of favor by agreeing to basic reforms. We can't let them take credit for this without holding them accountable."

Denise, the labor union leader, chimed in. "The city is good at dragging its feet. We've seen it before. They'll make a big announcement, but when it comes to implementing the changes, they'll stall or put up bureaucratic roadblocks. We need to keep the pressure on."

Danielle, always the strategist, leaned forward. "We need to establish a watchdog group—something independent from the city that tracks the implementation of the oversight board and the other reforms. We need to be able to point out every delay, every attempt to undercut the changes we fought for."

Aisha agreed. "And we need to keep organizing. The mayor's team thinks this will satisfy us, that we'll back off now that they've made these promises. We need to show them that this is just the beginning."

The group spent the next few days building a plan to ensure that the city followed through on its commitments. They reached out to their allies in other social justice organizations, labor unions, and community groups, creating a coalition that would monitor the city's progress on the oversight board and the promised community investments. They also held public forums to educate people on what the reforms should look like and what they could do if the city failed to deliver.

But as the weeks went on, Aisha could feel the strain of the fight taking its toll. The movement was growing, but so were the pressures from within and outside. People were tired. They had been fighting for months, and while the city's promises had given them a taste of victory, the reality of how slow change could be was starting to weigh on them.

One evening, after a long day of meetings and organizing, Aisha sat alone in her apartment, staring at her phone. The constant stream of calls, messages, and emails had become overwhelming. She hadn't had a moment to herself in weeks, and the weight of the movement felt heavier than ever. She knew she wasn't alone—her team was with her every step of the way—but the responsibility of leading this fight, of keeping everyone focused and united, was beginning to wear her down.

Jason noticed it too. He had been Aisha's closest confidant throughout the entire movement, and he could see the exhaustion in her eyes.

"You need a break," Jason said one night as they sat in the community center after a strategy meeting. "I know you feel like you have to carry all of this, but you can't keep going like this forever."

Aisha shook her head, her voice filled with a mix of frustration and determination. "I can't stop now. We're so close. If I back off, everything we've worked for could fall apart."

Jason's expression softened. "I get it. I really do. But you're no good to the movement if you're burned out. We've got a strong team. Let us carry some of the weight."

Aisha sighed, knowing he was right but struggling to let go of the control she felt she needed to maintain. "I just don't want to lose the momentum. We've been fighting so hard, and I can feel the system pushing back harder every day."

Jason nodded. "I know. But that's why we've got to pace ourselves. This fight isn't over, but it's not a sprint either. It's a marathon."

Aisha knew Jason was speaking from experience. He had been through these kinds of fights before—long, drawn-out battles where every inch of progress felt like a victory and a setback all at once. But she also knew that taking a step back, even for a moment, felt dangerous. The system they were fighting against was relentless, and any sign of weakness could give their opponents an opening.

But she also couldn't ignore her own exhaustion. The sleepless nights, the constant pressure, the never-ending meetings—it was all catching up to her.

A few days later, Aisha called another meeting with her core team. This time, the focus wasn't just on strategy but on sustainability. They needed to figure out how to keep the movement strong without burning themselves out.

"We need to build more leadership," Aisha said as they sat around the table. "I can't keep carrying this on my own, and neither can any of you. We need to train more people to step up, to take on leadership roles, so we can keep the movement going without killing ourselves in the process."

Malik agreed. "We've got a lot of people who are passionate about the cause, but they need direction. If we can train them, we can spread the workload and keep things moving."

Danielle, always thinking ahead, added, "We also need to build alliances with other groups who can help take the lead on certain issues. We don't have to do everything ourselves. There are other organizations fighting for the same things we are. We can share the load."

The group spent the next few weeks building out their leadership structure, identifying people within the movement who could take on more responsibility and helping them develop the skills they needed to lead. They also deepened their relationships with other social justice organizations, forming a network of support that allowed them to spread their efforts without losing focus.

But even as they worked to strengthen the movement, the city's leadership was finding new ways to delay the implementation of the promised reforms. The independent oversight board, which had been announced with fanfare, was now mired in bureaucratic red tape. The mayor's office claimed that they were "working through the details," but Aisha knew better. This was a tactic—stalling until the public's attention shifted elsewhere.

At one of their public forums, Denise stood up and addressed the crowd. "This is what they do. They make promises, then they drag their feet, hoping we'll forget or give up. But we're not going to let them get away with it."

The crowd erupted in applause, and Aisha felt a renewed sense of energy. They weren't going to give up. Not now. Not when they had come so far.

Aisha and her team ramped up their efforts, holding the city accountable at every turn. They organized marches, called out the delays in the media, and pressured city officials to move forward with the reforms they had promised. It was exhausting work, but it was necessary.

One night, after a particularly tense meeting with city officials, Aisha sat with Danielle and Jason at a local diner, nursing cups of coffee. The weight of the fight was still heavy on her shoulders, but for the first time in weeks, she allowed herself to feel a glimmer of hope.

"They're feeling the pressure," Danielle said, her voice filled with confidence. "They're trying to stall, but they know we're not going anywhere."

Jason nodded; his eyes sharp with determination. "They thought they could outlast us, but we've shown them that we're here to stay."

Aisha smiled, though her exhaustion was still evident. "We've held the line. Now we just must make sure we don't lose sight of the bigger picture."

As they left the diner that night, Aisha looked out at the city—the streets she had walked for years, the neighborhoods she had fought for, the people who had become her family in this struggle. The horizon still felt distant, but she knew they were getting closer. They had held the line through every obstacle, and now, they were ready for whatever came next.

Chapter 23: The Politics of Progress

As the movement continued to gain momentum, Aisha found herself navigating a new terrain—one that was as treacherous as it was unfamiliar: the world of politics. What had started as a grassroots movement demanding justice had grown into a force that the city's leadership could no longer ignore. But with that recognition came the realization that the fight for change wasn't just about protests and organizing; it was about power.

Aisha had always been wary of politicians. She had seen firsthand how promises were made in front of cameras, only to be broken behind closed doors. But now, she was being drawn into the very political system she had spent years fighting against. City officials who had once dismissed her were now calling for meetings, and community leaders with ties to the political establishment were reaching out to offer their support. It was an unsettling shift.

"You're becoming a power player," Jason said one evening as they sat in the community center, reviewing the latest proposals from city hall. "They see you as a threat, but they also see you as someone they need to work with. That gives us leverage, but it also comes with risks."

Aisha nodded, her mind racing with the implications. She had always believed in the power of the people to drive change, but now she was beginning to see that navigating the political landscape was just as important. The city's leaders weren't going to hand over power willingly—they would fight to keep control, even if that meant trying to co-opt the movement.

"They want to use us to legitimize their version of reform," Aisha said, her voice filled with frustration. "We have to be careful not to let them turn us into pawns in their political game."

The pressure to engage with the political establishment was growing, but Aisha knew that stepping into that world could come at a cost. The movement's strength had always been its independence, its refusal to play by the rules of the system they were trying to dismantle. But now, they were being forced to decide how far they were willing to go to achieve their goals.

Chapter 24: Walking the Line

The first signs of division within the movement began to emerge as they debated how to engage with the city's political establishment. Some members, particularly the younger activists like Marcus, were adamant that they should not compromise with a system they viewed as inherently corrupt. They argued that any engagement with the city's leadership would dilute the movement's message and undermine its legitimacy.

"We can't play their game," Marcus said during one of their strategy meetings. "If we start making deals with politicians, we're no better than they are. This movement was built on rejecting the system, not becoming part of it."

Others, like Denise and Danielle, saw things differently. They believed that engaging with the city's leadership, while fraught with challenges, was a necessary step toward achieving real change. They argued that if they refused to negotiate, they would lose the opportunity to influence policy and make lasting reforms.

"We can't afford to be idealistic," Danielle said. "We have the chance to shape the future of this city, but only if we're willing to engage with the people who hold the power. That doesn't mean we compromise our values—it means we're strategic about how we use our influence."

Aisha found herself caught between these two perspectives. She understood the importance of staying true to the movement's principles, but she also knew that real change required working within the system at some level. The question was how to do that without losing the movement's soul.

In the end, they decided to walk a delicate line—engaging with the political establishment, when necessary, but always on their terms. It was a strategy that required constant vigilance, but Aisha was determined to keep the movement's integrity intact.

Chapter 25: Divided Loyalties

As the movement grew more entangled in the city's power struggles, tensions within the coalition began to escalate. The strain of navigating the political landscape was taking its toll, and the once-unified front that had driven the movement was starting to show cracks.

Some members of the movement, particularly those with ties to more established community organizations, were eager to pursue opportunities for collaboration with the city's leadership. They believed that the movement's growing influence could be leveraged to secure funding and resources for their communities.

Others, like Marcus and the younger activists, felt increasingly alienated by what they saw as a shift toward compromise. They accused the movement's leaders of selling out, of losing sight of the radical vision that had sparked the protests in the first place.

"It feels like we're abandoning the people we're supposed to be fighting for," Marcus said one evening, his voice filled with frustration. "We started this movement to challenge the system, not to make deals with it."

Aisha listened, her heart heavy with the weight of the decisions they were making. She understood Marcus's anger, but she also knew that if they refused to engage with the city's leadership, they risked losing the opportunity to make real progress.

"We're not abandoning anyone," Aisha said, her voice firm. "But we have to be smart about how we fight. This isn't about making deals—it's about using every tool we have to dismantle the system from the inside out."

But the divisions within the movement were growing, and Aisha knew that if they didn't find a way to bridge the gap, the movement could fracture.

Chapter 26: The Price of Compromise

The more Aisha and her team engaged with the city's leadership, the more they realized that every victory came with a cost. The oversight board they had fought so hard to establish was moving forward, but the city was dragging its feet on other key reforms, particularly those related to community investment and housing.

As they continued to push for these changes, they found themselves facing increased resistance from both the political establishment and some members of their own coalition. The city's leaders, while willing to make concessions on policing, were reluctant to commit to the kind of structural changes that would address the deeper issues of inequality and poverty.

At the same time, some members of the movement began to question whether the compromises they were making were worth the limited gains they were achieving. The more they engaged with the system, the more they risked being co-opted by it.

"We're giving up too much," Marcus said during one particularly heated meeting. "We've become part of the very system we're supposed to be fighting."

Aisha felt the weight of his words, but she also knew that they had no choice but to keep pushing forward. The stakes were too high, and the communities they were fighting for couldn't afford to wait for perfect solutions.

"This isn't about compromising our values," Aisha said. "It's about getting as much as we can while we have the leverage. But we're not done. We're never done."

Chapter 27: A Growing Movement, A Growing Threat

As the movement's influence continued to grow, so did the backlash from those who saw their power as a threat. The police union, local business leaders, and conservative political groups ramped up their efforts to discredit the movement, launching smear campaigns and working to undermine the reforms they had fought for.

The attacks came from all sides—media outlets sympathetic to the police painted the movement as dangerous radicals, while business leaders warned that the movement's demands would lead to economic instability. Aisha herself became a target, receiving threats and facing relentless scrutiny from the press.

"They're scared," Jason said one evening after a particularly vicious article was published about Aisha. "They're doing everything they can to tear you down because they know you're winning."

Aisha nodded, though the constant attacks were taking their toll. "I knew this would happen. But it doesn't make it any easier."

Despite the growing opposition, the movement continued to push forward, organizing larger protests and rallies, building alliances with national organizations, and keeping the pressure on the city's leadership. But Aisha knew that the more successful they became, the more dangerous their enemies would become.

Chapter 28: The Battle for Public Opinion

The fight for justice was no longer just a battle in the streets or in the halls of city government—it was a battle for the hearts and minds of the public. As the movement grew, so did the efforts to sway public opinion, both in their favor and against them.

Aisha and her team worked tirelessly to shape the narrative, using social media, interviews, and public forums to communicate their message and counter the attacks from their opponents. They knew that if they lost the public's support, they would lose their leverage in the fight for reform.

But the opposition was just as determined. The police union and their allies in the media flooded the airwaves with stories about rising crime rates, blaming the movement for destabilizing the city. Business leaders warned that the movement's demands for higher wages and affordable housing would drive businesses out of the city, leading to economic collapse.

Aisha felt the pressure mounting, but she refused to back down. "We're not just fighting for policy changes," she said during one interview. "We're fighting to change the way people see justice, equality, and what's possible for our communities. This isn't just about politics—it's about building a future where everyone has a chance to thrive.

Chapter 29: The Breaking Point

As the pressure on the movement reached its peak, so did the tensions within the coalition. The divisions that had been simmering for months finally boiled over as disagreements about strategy, tactics, and the direction of the movement came to a head.

Marcus and the younger activists, frustrated by what they saw as the movement's growing compromises, began organizing their own actions—more radical protests and direct actions that put them in direct conflict with the city's leadership. They accused Aisha and her team of selling out, of losing sight of the movement's original vision.

"We can't keep playing by their rules," Marcus said during one heated argument. "We need to take the fight to them, not wait for permission to make change."

Aisha, exhausted by the constant pressure, tried to hold the coalition together. "We're all fighting for the same thing," she said. "But if we start fighting each other, we're going to lose everything we've built."

But the fractures were becoming harder to ignore. The movement that had once been unified was now pulling in different directions, and Aisha knew that if they couldn't find a way to reconcile, the movement could collapse.

Chapter 30: A New Vision

As the movement stood on the brink of fracture, Aisha knew they needed a new path forward—a way to unite the coalition without compromising their core values. It was a daunting task, but she refused to let the movement fall apart.

Over the next few weeks, Aisha and her core team worked tirelessly to rebuild trust within the coalition, holding difficult conversations and finding common ground between the different factions. They brought in mediators, held community meetings, and focused on healing the divisions that had emerged.

But they also recognized that the movement needed a new vision—one that acknowledged the complexities of the fight ahead while staying true to the radical spirit that had driven them from the beginning. They crafted a new set of principles, one that balanced the need for immediate reforms with a long-term vision for systemic change.

It wasn't easy, and the road ahead was still filled with challenges. But as Aisha stood before the coalition, outlining their new vision, she felt a renewed sense of hope.

"This movement was never just about winning one battle," Aisha said, her voice strong and clear. "It's about building a future where justice isn't just a word, but a reality for everyone. And we're not done yet."

The coalition stood united once again, ready to face whatever came next.

Chapter 31: Into the Storm

The movement was stronger than ever, but so was the opposition. Aisha could feel it in the way the city's leaders spoke about the reforms, in the way business leaders continued to fund anti-reform campaigns, and in the ever-present tension between her coalition and the police. Despite the victories they had won, the battle was far from over. If anything, the stakes were higher now. The storm that had been brewing for months was about to hit, and Aisha knew they had to be ready.

The attacks from the opposition became more vicious and targeted. Media outlets sympathetic to the police and business elite ran smear campaigns against the movement, painting them as radicals bent on tearing the city apart. Anonymous threats became more frequent, and Aisha found herself looking over her shoulder more than ever. There was a sense that the opposition was growing desperate, but that desperation made them more dangerous.

One morning, as Aisha was leaving her apartment, she noticed something that made her heart race: a black SUV, the kind that had been parked outside her building before, idling on the corner. She'd seen it enough times to know it wasn't just a coincidence. She could feel the eyes on her, watching, waiting.

"They're trying to intimidate you," Jason said when she told him about it later that day. "It's not going to work."

Aisha nodded, but the sense of unease lingered. "They're not just watching me. They're waiting for us to slip up, waiting for any excuse to come down on us harder."

Jason leaned back in his chair; his expression serious. "Then we make sure we don't give them one."

But staying on the defensive wasn't enough. The movement had to keep pushing, even as the storm around them intensified. Aisha and her team organized more protests, more community meetings, and more public forums to keep the pressure on the city. They couldn't afford to let the opposition control the narrative.

As they prepared for their next major protest—one that was set to coincide with a key vote on police oversight reforms in the city council—Aisha felt the weight of the moment pressing down on her. This vote was critical. If the reforms passed, it would solidify the oversight board's power and ensure that the city couldn't backtrack on the promises it had made. If the vote failed, it would be a devastating blow, one that could set the movement back months, if not years.

"We have to be ready for anything," Aisha told her team during their final strategy meeting before the protest. "The police are going to be out in force, and the opposition is going to do everything they can to undermine us. We can't give them any reason to shut us down."

Jason, ever the strategist, had already mapped out the security measures they would take to protect the protesters. They had legal observers on standby, medics ready in case things got violent, and a communications team monitoring social media to keep the public informed in real-time.

"We've covered all our bases," Jason said, his voice steady. "But we need to be prepared for the worst."

Aisha nodded, her mind racing with everything that could go wrong. The storm was coming, and all they could do was stand their ground.

Chapter 32: When the Streets Speak

The day of the protest dawned with a heavy, oppressive sky, mirroring the tension in the air. Thousands of people had gathered, filling the streets in front of city hall. Aisha stood at the front, megaphone in hand, watching as the crowd swelled around her. The energy was palpable, a mix of anger, hope, and determination.

"We're here because they can't ignore us anymore," Aisha shouted into the megaphone, her voice carrying over the crowd. "They've tried to silence us, to shut us down, but we're still standing. Today, we demand justice. We demand accountability. And we won't leave until they hear us."

The crowd roared in response, their chants echoing through the streets. It was a powerful sight—thousands of people, from all walks of life, united in their fight for change. But even as Aisha felt the surge of hope, she knew that the opposition was watching, waiting for any opportunity to strike.

The police presence was overwhelming. Rows of officers in riot gear lined the streets, their faces obscured by helmets, their hands resting on batons. The tension between the protesters and the police was electric, and Aisha could feel it in the way the crowd moved, in the way people glanced nervously at the officers. One wrong move, and the situation could spiral out of control.

As the protest wore on, Aisha kept a close eye on the crowd, her instincts on high alert. She knew they had to maintain control—any violence, any chaos, and the police would use it as an excuse to shut them down. But despite their efforts to keep things peaceful, there was an undercurrent of anger in the air, and Aisha could sense that not everyone in the crowd was there for the same reasons.

Suddenly, a commotion broke out near the back of the protest. A small group of agitators—faces obscured by masks—began throwing rocks and bottles at the police. The officers responded immediately, charging into the crowd with batons raised, and chaos erupted.

"Stay calm!" Aisha shouted into the megaphone, trying to regain control of the situation. "This is what they want. Don't let them turn this into a riot."

But it was too late. The police had already moved in, and the peaceful protest quickly devolved into chaos. Tear gas filled the air, and Aisha could hear the shouts of panic as protesters scrambled to escape the onslaught.

Jason appeared at her side, pulling her back as the police advanced. "We need to get out of here," he said urgently. "They're going to start making arrests."

Aisha nodded, her heart pounding as they retreated from the front lines. The streets were filled with smoke and confusion, and she could barely make out the figures of the police and protesters clashing in the haze. It was exactly what she had feared—the opposition had found their excuse, and now the protest was spiraling out of control.

Chapter 33: The Aftermath

In the days following the protest, the city was in turmoil. The images of police clashing with protesters, of tear gas filling the streets and people being arrested, dominated the news. The media had a field day, with some outlets portraying the protesters as violent agitators and others condemning the police for their brutal response.

Aisha's heart sank as she watched the coverage. They had worked so hard to keep the protest peaceful, but the actions of a few had given the opposition exactly what they wanted. The city's leaders wasted no time using the chaos as an excuse to delay the vote on the police reforms, citing "public safety concerns."

"We can't let this be the end," Aisha said during a tense meeting with her team. "They're going to try to use this to discredit us, to paint us as violent radicals. We need to push back harder than ever."

But even as they regrouped, Aisha knew that the protest had taken a toll on the movement. Some members were disillusioned by the violence, while others felt betrayed by the city's response. The fractures that had been simmering within the coalition began to widen, and Aisha struggled to keep everyone focused on the bigger picture.

"We're not done," Aisha said, her voice firm. "We knew this fight would be long and hard, but we can't stop now. We've come too far to give up."

Chapter 34: A Moment of Reckoning

As the dust settled from the protest, Aisha found herself at a crossroads. The movement had gained national attention, but the cost had been high. The city's leadership was using the chaos as a pretext to stall the reforms, and the police union was more emboldened than ever. At the same time, the movement's internal divisions were becoming harder to ignore.

Aisha knew that they had to decide. They could either continue pushing forward, risking more confrontations with the police and the city's leadership, or they could shift their focus to other strategies—legal battles, community organizing, and coalition-building.

"We need to be smart about this," Danielle said during one of their strategy meetings. "The protest showed us how far they're willing to go to shut us down. We can't keep playing into their hands."

Jason agreed. "We need to take the fight to a different level. The streets aren't the only place we can make change."

Aisha listened, her mind racing with the possibilities. She knew they couldn't afford another chaotic protest, but she also knew that they couldn't let the momentum die. They had to find a new way forward.

Chapter 35: Building Power from Within

In the weeks that followed, Aisha and her team shifted their focus. They knew that the streets were no longer safe for large-scale protests, at least for the time being, so they turned their attention to building power from within. They organized community meetings, reaching out to local leaders and neighborhood organizations to build a network of support that could withstand the opposition's attacks.

"We need to build something that can't be torn down by one protest," Aisha said during one of their meetings. "We need to create a movement that's so deeply rooted in the community that no amount of tear gas or arrests can stop it."

The strategy worked. As they strengthened their ties to the community, more people began to see the movement not just as a protest group, but as a force for real, lasting change. They held workshops on civil rights, organized voter registration drives, and worked with local businesses to support their efforts.

But even as they built power from within, Aisha knew that the political battle was far from over. The city's leadership was still dragging its feet on the police reforms, and the opposition was growing more desperate.

Chapter 36: The Long Game

By now, Aisha had come to understand that the fight for justice was not a series of short battles but a long, drawn-out war. Every victory was hard-won, and every setback felt like a blow to the movement's morale. But they had to keep going.

The next few months were marked by tireless work. Aisha and her team continued to build their network of allies, expanding their reach beyond the city to other movements across the country. They worked with national civil rights organizations, forming coalitions that gave them the resources and support they needed to continue their fight.

At the same time, they kept the pressure on the city, using legal avenues to push for the reforms that had been delayed. They filed lawsuits, lobbied city council members, and organized smaller, targeted protests that kept the public's attention on the issue without inviting the same level of violence.

It was a slow, grinding process, but Aisha knew that this was how real change happened—not in a single, dramatic moment, but through years of sustained effort.

Chapter 37: A Victory in Sight

After months of relentless pressure, the city finally announced that it would move forward with the vote on the police reforms. It was a moment of triumph for Aisha and her team—a sign that their efforts were paying off.

The day of the vote was tense. Aisha and her coalition had worked tirelessly to secure enough votes from the city council to pass the reforms, but they knew that anything could happen. The police union was still fighting tooth and nail to block the reforms, and business leaders were applying pressure behind the scenes.

As Aisha sat in the gallery, watching the council members file in, she felt a mixture of hope and anxiety. This was the moment they had been working toward for so long, and it was finally within reach.

When the final vote came in, the reforms passed by a narrow margin. The oversight board would be established, with the power to investigate police misconduct and hold officers accountable.

The room erupted in applause, but Aisha sat in stunned silence, the weight of the moment crashing over her. They had done it. They had won.

Chapter 38: The Aftermath of Victory

The moment the vote passed; Aisha felt an overwhelming surge of relief. For months, she and her team had fought relentlessly for this victory, and now, they had secured it. The police reforms would go into effect, and the independent oversight board they had fought so hard to establish would have real power to hold officers accountable. It was a moment of triumph, but as Aisha sat in the council chamber, watching her team celebrate, she couldn't shake the feeling that this was only the beginning.

The victory was real, but so were the challenges that lay ahead. The oversight board, while a major step forward, wasn't a panacea. It would take time for the board to be set up and for the reforms to take effect, and Aisha knew that the police union and other opponents would do everything they could to undermine its power.

Later that night, as she walked home from the council meeting, Aisha allowed herself a moment of quiet reflection. The streets were still buzzing with energy from the day's events, but for the first time in a long time, Aisha felt a sense of calm. They had achieved something monumental, but there was still so much work to do.

When she reached her apartment, she found Jason waiting for her, his face lit with a mixture of pride and exhaustion.

"We did it," Jason said, pulling her into a hug. "You did it."

Aisha smiled, but there was a heaviness in her voice when she replied. "We did it together. But this is just the start. Now we must make sure they actually follow through."

Jason nodded, understanding the weight of what she was feeling. "I know. But tonight, let's take a moment to celebrate. We've earned it."

Chapter 39: Navigating New Terrain

In the weeks following the victory, Aisha and her team found themselves in unfamiliar territory. For so long, they had been fighting to win the vote on police reforms, and now that they had, the focus shifted to ensuring that the reforms were implemented properly. It was a new phase of the fight—one that required patience, persistence, and a deep understanding of how the city's bureaucracy worked.

Danielle took the lead on tracking the implementation of the oversight board, working closely with legal experts and community organizations to ensure that the board would have the resources and authority it needed to be effective. Aisha and Jason, meanwhile, continued to organize public forums and community meetings to keep the movement engaged and informed.

"We can't let people think the fight is over just because we won the vote," Aisha said during one of their strategy sessions. "If we don't stay on top of this, they'll drag their feet, and the reforms will be watered down."

Denise agreed. "We need to keep the pressure on. The oversight board is a win, but it's only as powerful as we make it. If the city stalls or cuts funding, we'll be right back where we started."

Aisha knew they were entering a critical phase. The battle for the vote had been high-profile, filled with protests and media attention. But now, the fight was moving behind closed doors, into the realm of policy implementation and bureaucratic negotiations. It was a different kind of challenge, one that required a new set of skills.

But Aisha was ready. They had fought too hard to let the system take this victory away.

Chapter 40: A Movement Transformed

As the months passed, Aisha could feel the movement evolving. What had started as a grassroots effort to demand justice had grown into something much larger. The coalition they had built was stronger than ever, and their influence extended far beyond the city's borders. National organizations were reaching out, offering support and resources, and other cities were beginning to look to their movement as a model for how to fight for police reform.

But with that growth came new challenges. The movement was no longer just a group of activists fighting for change—it was now a political force, one that had to navigate the complexities of power, influence, and public perception. Aisha found herself in meetings with politicians, community leaders, and national organizations, trying to balance the movement's radical roots with the realities of working within the system.

"It's strange, isn't it?" Jason said one evening as they prepared for a meeting with a national civil rights organization. "We've gone from protesting in the streets to sitting in boardrooms, negotiating with people we used to fight against."

Aisha smiled, though there was a hint of uncertainty in her eyes. "It is strange. But I think this is what we've been working toward. We wanted power—to make real, lasting change. This is what that looks like."

But even as Aisha embraced the movement's new role, she was careful not to lose sight of the values that had driven them from the beginning. She knew that power could corrupt, and she was determined to keep the movement grounded in its commitment to justice, equality, and accountability.

"We have to stay true to who we are," Aisha said during a leadership meeting. "Just because we're gaining influence doesn't mean we compromise on our principles. We're here to dismantle the system, not become part of it."

Chapter 41: The Burden of Leadership

With the movement's growing influence came a growing burden for Aisha. She had always been the face of the fight for justice, but now that role came with new pressures. Every decision she made was scrutinized, not just by the opposition, but by her own allies. There were constant demands for her time—interviews, meetings, public appearances—and the weight of it all was beginning to take a toll.

Jason had noticed the change in her. Aisha was always the first to arrive at meetings and the last to leave, but lately, she seemed more tired, more withdrawn. She carried the weight of the movement on her shoulders, and Jason worried that it was starting to break her down.

"You need to take a step back," Jason said one night as they walked through the neighborhood, trying to escape the constant demands of the movement. "You've been running yourself into the ground for months. It's okay to let other people carry some of the weight."

Aisha shook her head, her voice filled with quiet determination. "I can't stop now. There's too much at stake."

"I know," Jason said, his tone gentle. "But you're not in this alone. You've built a team—trust them to lead too. If you burn out, the whole movement suffers."

Aisha knew Jason was right. The fight had consumed her life for so long that she didn't know how to take a step back. But she also knew that if she didn't, the pressure could break her. Leadership was a heavy burden, and Aisha was beginning to understand just how much it cost.

Chapter 42: The Politics of Compromise

As Aisha navigated the complexities of leadership, she found herself facing another challenge: the politics of compromise. While the oversight board was a major victory, the city's leadership was still resistant to many of the other reforms the movement had been pushing for, particularly around housing, education, and healthcare. Aisha was being pulled into negotiations with city officials, where every gain seemed to come with a trade-off.

"They're offering us more funding for community programs," Danielle said during one meeting, "but they're refusing to commit to any meaningful changes in housing policy."

Aisha felt a wave of frustration. "So, they want to keep throwing money at the problem without addressing the root causes."

Danielle nodded. "Exactly. They want to give us just enough to keep us quiet, without changing the system."

Aisha had always known that the fight for justice would be filled with compromises, but now that she was in the middle of it, the reality was harder to accept. Every time they won a victory, it seemed to come with a cost—a concession that chipped away at the movement's larger vision for systemic change.

"We can't accept their half-measures," Aisha said. "We need to keep pushing for real change, even if it takes longer."

But even as Aisha made that commitment, she knew that the politics of compromise would be an ongoing struggle. The city's leaders were experts at deflecting, delaying, and offering just enough to make it seem like progress was being made. Aisha had to find a way to navigate those waters without losing sight of the movement's ultimate goals.

Chapter 43: A New Generation Rising

As the movement continued to evolve, Aisha began to notice a shift. The younger activists who had joined the movement early on—people like Marcus—were stepping into leadership roles of their own. They were organizing protests, leading community meetings, and pushing for more radical change. Aisha was proud of them, but she also sensed that their vision for the movement was different from hers.

"They're hungry for change, and they're not willing to wait," Jason said one evening as they discussed the younger activists. "I get it. We were the same way when we started."

Aisha smiled, remembering the early days of the movement, when they had been filled with the same fire and determination. "I'm proud of them. They're going to take this movement places we never imagined."

But even as she embraced the rise of a new generation of leaders, Aisha knew that the movement was changing. The younger activists were less willing to engage with the political system, more focused on direct action and radical transformation. It was a tension that had always been present in the movement, but now it was becoming more pronounced.

"We need to find a balance," Aisha said. "We can't abandon the fight in the streets, but we also can't ignore the gains we've made by engaging with the system."

It was a delicate balancing act, one that required constant negotiation and communication. But Aisha believed that the movement was strong enough to hold both approaches—to fight for immediate change while keeping their eyes on the long-term goal of dismantling the system.

Chapter 44: The Long Road Ahead

As Aisha stood at the edge of the movement she had helped build, she knew that the fight for justice was far from over. They had won major victories—police reforms, community investments, national recognition—but the deeper, systemic changes they were fighting for would take years, if not decades, to achieve.

The road ahead was long, and there would be setbacks, betrayals, and compromises along the way. But Aisha was no longer fighting alone. The movement had grown beyond her, carried by a new generation of leaders who were just as committed to justice as she was.

As she looked out at the faces of the people who had become her family in this fight, Aisha felt a sense of hope. They had come so far, and they weren't done yet.

"We've built something powerful," Aisha said during a leadership meeting. "Something that will outlast us. And as long as we keep fighting, as long as we stay true to our vision, we're going to change the world."

The movement stood at a crossroads, ready to face whatever challenges lay ahead. And Aisha knew that no matter how long the road, they would keep walking it together.

Chapter 45: A New Battle Emerges

Just as Aisha and her team were beginning to see the fruits of their labor with the implementation of police reforms, another storm began brewing on the horizon: the housing crisis. For years, the city had been quietly selling off public land to developers, driving up rent prices and pushing out long-time residents. Gentrification had become a silent force in the background of the movement, but now, it was impossible to ignore. People were losing their homes, neighborhoods were being transformed, and the same communities that had fought for police reform were now battling displacement.

The housing crisis had always been on the movement's radar, but with so much of their focus on police reform, it had taken a backseat. Now, it was clear that this issue needed their full attention.

"We can't talk about justice without talking about housing," Aisha said during one of their strategy meetings. "People can't fight for change if they're worried about losing their homes. We need to take this on."

Jason nodded; his face grim. "Developers have been running wild for years, and the city has been complicit. If we don't stop them, there won't be anything left of these communities."

Aisha knew that this battle would be different from the one they had fought for police reform. The forces driving gentrification were deeply embedded in the city's economy, tied to powerful developers and wealthy investors. This wasn't just about policies—it was about money, and a lot of it.

But the stakes couldn't be higher. If they didn't fight back, the communities they had fought to protect would be wiped out, replaced by luxury condos and high-end shops. It was a battle for survival, and Aisha was ready to lead the charge.

Chapter 46: The Fight for Home

The first step was organizing the people who were directly affected. Aisha and her team began by holding community meetings in neighborhoods that were being hit hardest by rising rents and displacement. They listened to the stories of residents who had lived in the city for decades, only to be pushed out by developers who saw their homes as investments, not as places where families lived and grew.

At one meeting, an elderly woman named Mrs. Thompson stood up, her voice shaking with anger and fear. "I've lived in this house for 40 years," she said. "Raised my children here, and now they're telling me I have to leave because they want to build some fancy new apartment building. Where am I supposed to go? How is that fair?"

Aisha's heart broke as she listened to Mrs. Thompson's story. It was one of many she had heard in recent weeks. Families, elderly residents, low-income workers—people who had built their lives in these neighborhoods were being forced out, and no one seemed to care.

"We're not going to let them take your home," Aisha said, her voice filled with determination. "We're going to fight this, and we're going to win."

The movement's focus shifted to housing justice. They began organizing protests outside city hall, demanding that the city stop selling public land to developers and pass rent control measures to protect tenants. They worked with housing advocates and legal experts to draft proposals that would limit the power of developers and prioritize affordable housing.

But the opposition was fierce. The developers had deep pockets and powerful allies in city government. They fought back hard, funding smear campaigns against the movement and spreading fear that rent control would destroy the city's economy.

"We're up against a different kind of enemy this time," Danielle said during one of their strategy meetings. "Developers have money, and they're not afraid to use it. They're going to fight us every step of the way."

Aisha nodded. "Let them fight. We've taken on powerful forces before, and we'll do it again. This is about more than just housing—it's about the right to live with dignity in your own community."

Chapter 47: A City Divided

As the housing battle heated up, the city became more polarized than ever. On one side were the developers, backed by wealthy investors and the political elite. They argued that new development was necessary for the city's growth and that limiting their ability to build would hurt the economy. On the other side were the residents, led by Aisha and her coalition, who saw the development as nothing more than a land grab that was destroying the fabric of their communities.

The city council was split. Some members, pressured by their constituents, supported the movement's calls for rent control and affordable housing. Others, backed by developers, argued that the movement's demands were unrealistic and would stifle economic growth.

"We're walking a tightrope here," Jason said one evening as they prepared for a public hearing on the housing proposals. "If we push too hard, we risk losing the support we've built. But if we don't push hard enough, nothing will change."

Aisha knew that they were in a precarious position. The housing crisis was a deeply emotional issue, and it was easy for people to get caught up in the fear of change. The developers were using that fear to their advantage, flooding the airwaves with ads that warned of job losses and economic collapse if the movement's proposals were passed.

But Aisha wasn't swayed. She knew that this fight was about more than just numbers and development plans—it was about people's lives.

"We have to keep reminding them what this is really about," Aisha said. "This isn't just about housing policy—it's about justice. It's about people being able to stay in their homes and live in the communities they've built.

Chapter 48: Taking the Fight to the Streets

The fight for housing justice took on a new intensity as Aisha and her team organized a massive march through the heart of the city. Tens of thousands of people turned out, holding signs that read "Homes Not Hotels" and "Stop Displacement Now." The energy was electric, a powerful reminder of the strength of the movement.

As Aisha stood at the front of the march, looking out over the sea of people, she felt a surge of pride. They had come so far, and now they were taking the fight to the next level.

"We're not just fighting for housing," Aisha said into the megaphone as the crowd gathered outside city hall. "We're fighting for the soul of this city. We're fighting for the right to live with dignity, for the right to stay in the communities we've built. And we're not going anywhere."

The march sent a clear message to the city's leaders: the people were not backing down. But Aisha knew that the real battle was happening behind the scenes, in the city council chambers and in the offices of developers who were scrambling to protect their interests.

"We've got the public on our side," Danielle said after the march. "But the developers are working overtime to block us. We need to be ready for whatever they throw at us next."

Chapter 49: The Power of Community

One of the most powerful aspects of the housing fight was the way it brought people together. The movement had always been about community, but now, that sense of solidarity was stronger than ever. People who had never been involved in activism before were stepping up, organizing their neighbors, attending city council meetings, and sharing their stories.

Mrs. Thompson, the elderly woman who had spoken out at one of the early community meetings, became one of the movement's most passionate advocates. She rallied her neighbors, spoke at public forums, and even appeared on local news programs, sharing her story of displacement and fighting for her right to stay in her home.

"I never thought I'd be doing this," Mrs. Thompson said one afternoon as she stood beside Aisha at a rally. "But this is my home. And I'm not going to let anyone take it from me."

Aisha smiled, feeling a deep sense of pride in the people who had risen to the occasion. This was what the movement was all about—people coming together, standing up for each other, and refusing to back down.

Chapter 50: A Hard-Won Victory

After months of tireless organizing, protests, and negotiations, the city council finally voted on the housing proposals. It was a tense day, with both sides packing the council chambers and the media closely watching the outcome.

When the final vote was announced, the movement's proposals for rent control and affordable housing passed by a slim margin. It was a hard-won victory, but a victory, nonetheless.

As the crowd outside city hall erupted in cheers, Aisha felt a mixture of relief and exhaustion. They had won another battle, but the war was far from over. The developers would continue to fight, and the forces of gentrification were still powerful. But for now, they had secured a major victory for the people who needed it most.

Later that night, as Aisha and her team celebrated with their supporters, she reflected on how far they had come. The fight for housing justice had been brutal, but they had shown that when people came together, they could win—even against the most powerful forces.

"We've won today," Aisha said as she raised a glass in a toast. "But the fight isn't over. We'll keep going, keep pushing, until everyone has a place to call home."

Chapter 51: A New Frontline

With the housing battle behind them, Aisha and her team turned their attention to another critical issue plaguing the city: education. For years, the public school system had been neglected, underfunded, and allowed to deteriorate. The same communities that had fought against police brutality and displacement were also suffering from a broken education system that left their children behind.

Aisha had always known that the fight for justice had to include education. It was the foundation of opportunity, and without it, everything else they were fighting for—economic justice, housing, police reform—would be meaningless.

"Our kids are being failed," Aisha said during one of their first strategy meetings on education reform. "They're being set up for failure from the moment they walk into those schools. This is the next fight we have to take on."

Jason, who had grown up attending the city's public schools, was particularly passionate about this issue. He had seen firsthand how underfunded schools led to a cycle of poverty and inequality. "I made it out, but a lot of my friends didn't. The system is designed to keep people down, and it's our kids who suffer the most."

The challenges were immense. The school system was underfunded, teachers were overworked and underpaid, and the infrastructure in many schools was crumbling. But perhaps the biggest challenge was the deeply entrenched inequality that had left certain neighborhoods with well-resourced schools while others were left with overcrowded classrooms and outdated materials.

"This isn't just about fixing broken schools," Aisha said. "This is about dismantling the systemic racism and inequality that have been baked into our education system for decades."

Chapter 52: Education on the Edge

The first step was gathering data. Aisha and her team began by conducting a series of community forums, where parents, students, and teachers shared their experiences with the public school system. What they heard was heartbreaking: overcrowded classrooms, broken-down facilities, a lack of textbooks, and a school-to-prison pipeline that funneled too many young Black and brown children out of the classroom and into the criminal justice system.

"We're asking our teachers to work miracles with nothing," said Mr. Jackson, a high school teacher who had been working in the city for over 20 years. "These kids have so much potential, but they're being ignored. The system is set up to fail them."

Aisha and her team compiled the stories, statistics, and experiences into a detailed report that painted a stark picture of educational inequality in the city. The report became the foundation of their campaign for education reform. They demanded more funding for public schools, better pay for teachers, updated facilities, and an end to punitive policies that criminalized students instead of supporting them.

But just like in the housing fight, they knew they were up against powerful forces. Wealthy neighborhoods had well-funded schools, and their residents didn't want to see resources diverted to other areas. The city's political leaders were hesitant to take on the issue, fearing backlash from affluent voters and the wealthy donors who funded their campaigns.

"This isn't going to be easy," Danielle said. "The people who benefit from the current system aren't going to give up their privilege without a fight."

Aisha nodded, her face set with determination. "Then we'll fight."

Chapter 53: Students Rising

One of the most powerful aspects of the battle of education was the way it empowered students to become activists. As Aisha and her team organized town halls and rallies, students from across the city began to speak out about their experiences.

At one rally, a 16-year-old student named Maya stood in front of the crowd, her voice filled with emotion. "We're not just numbers. We're not just kids you can ignore. We deserve better. We deserve a chance to succeed."

Maya's speech went viral, and she quickly became one of the faces of the movement. She spoke at city council meetings, gave interviews to the press, and organized protests outside her school. Her passion and determination inspired students across the city to act, and soon, a wave of student-led activism was sweeping through the city's schools.

"This is our future," Maya said during one of her speeches. "We're fighting for our right to learn, to grow, to have a chance. And we're not going to stop until we get it."

The students' voices added a new level of urgency to the movement. It wasn't just parents and teachers fighting for change—it was the very people who were being failed by the system. Aisha knew that this was the key to winning the fight: empowering the students to lead the charge.

Chapter 54: The Battle for Funding

As the education movement gained momentum, the question of funding became the central issue. The city's public schools were severely underfunded, but the political will to allocate more resources was lacking. Wealthy residents, whose children attended private schools or well-resourced public schools, were resistant to any tax increases that would fund the city's struggling schools.

"We've got the money," Jason said during a strategy meeting. "It's just being spent in the wrong places. We need to make sure people understand that this is about priorities. If we don't invest in education now, we're going to pay for it later."

Aisha and her team launched a campaign to push for increased funding for public schools, targeting both the city's political leaders and the wealthy residents who were opposed to change. They organized marches, held press conferences, and released their report to the media, framing the issue as one of moral responsibility.

But the opposition was fierce. Business leaders argued that raising taxes would hurt the city's economy, and conservative media outlets ran stories claiming that the movement's demands were unrealistic and would bankrupt the city.

"They're trying to scare people," Aisha said. "But we can't let fear stop us. This is about our kids' futures, and we're not going to back down."

Chapter 55: Teachers on the Frontline

While the students were leading the charge, the teachers were the backbone of the movement. They had been fighting for better pay, better resources, and better working conditions for years, and now, they saw an opportunity to finally make real change.

At the center of the teachers' fight was Ms. Rodriguez, a beloved elementary school teacher who had been working in one of the city's poorest neighborhoods for over 25 years. She had seen the effects of underfunding firsthand, watching as her students struggled with outdated textbooks and crumbling facilities.

"We're being asked to do the impossible," Ms. Rodriguez said during a city council meeting. "We can't keep asking teachers to make up for the failures of the system. We need support. We need resources. And most of all, we need to stop treating education like it's something that can be sacrificed."

Ms. Rodriguez's words resonated deeply, and she became one of the movement's most vocal advocates. She organized teacher walkouts, led rallies, and worked with Aisha's team to push the city council to take action.

"Teachers are the frontline of this fight," Aisha said. "They're the ones who see the effects of this broken system every day, and we need to stand with them."

Chapter 56: A Critical Vote

After months of organizing, protesting, and negotiating, the movement's fight for education reform came down to a critical vote in the city council. The council was set to vote on a series of measures that would increase funding for public schools, raise teacher salaries, and allocate resources for much-needed repairs to school facilities.

The opposition, led by business leaders and conservative politicians, was pushing hard to block the measures, arguing that they would cripple the city's budget. But Aisha and her team had mobilized an army of parents, students, and teachers to pressure the council into doing the right thing.

The day of the vote was tense. The council chambers were packed with supporters and opponents of the measures, and the air was thick with anticipation. As Aisha sat with her team, watching the council members file in, she felt a familiar mix of hope and anxiety.

"This is it," Jason said quietly. "We've done everything we can. Now we just have to wait."

The vote was close, but when the final tally was announced, the education reform measures passed by a slim margin. The room erupted in cheers, and Aisha felt a wave of relief wash over her. They had done it. They had won.

Later that evening, as Aisha stood outside city hall, surrounded by students, teachers, and parents who had fought so hard for this victory, she felt a deep sense of pride. They had taken on one of the city's most deeply entrenched problems, and they had won.

"We've made history today," Aisha said as she addressed the crowd. "But this is just the beginning. Our fight for justice, for equality, for the future of our children—it doesn't end here. We've won this battle, but the war for a better future is far from over.

Chapter 57: Health and Healing

With the victory in education reform still fresh, Aisha and her team set their sights on a new challenge: healthcare. The same communities that had been fighting for justice in policing, housing, and education were also grappling with a lack of access to quality healthcare. Hospitals in poor neighborhoods were underfunded, clinics were overcrowded, and many residents had to travel miles to receive basic care. The healthcare system, like the education and housing systems, was deeply unequal, and Aisha knew that this fight was just as crucial.

"We can't talk about justice if people are being denied healthcare," Aisha said during one of their early meetings on the issue. "Our communities are suffering people are dying because they don't have access to the care they need. We need to fix this."

The healthcare crisis had always been in the background of their other battles, but now it was time to confront it head-on. The fight would not only be about hospitals and clinics but also about addressing the systemic inequalities that had long contributed to health disparities in marginalized communities.

Jason, who had lost family members due to inadequate healthcare, was passionate about this fight. "This isn't just about doctors and nurses—it's about the system that decides who gets care and who doesn't. We're up against the insurance companies, the pharmaceutical industry, and the politicians who protect them."

Aisha knew that the healthcare battle would be complex and multifaceted, but she also knew it was one they couldn't afford to lose.

Chapter 58: Health in Crisis

The first step in the healthcare fight was identifying the key issues that were affecting the community. Aisha and her team organized a series of town halls and listening sessions, where residents shared their experiences with the healthcare system. What they heard was devastating: people who couldn't afford their medications, mothers who had to take multiple buses to get their children to a doctor, elderly residents who went without care because they didn't have insurance.

One story that struck Aisha deeply was that of a young woman named Nadia, who had been battling chronic illness for years without adequate medical support.

"I go to the emergency room because it's the only place I can get help," Nadia said, her voice shaking. "But they just patch me up and send me home. I can't afford the treatments I need, and no one seems to care. I feel like I'm being left to die."

Nadia's story echoed those of many others in the community—people who were falling through the cracks of a broken healthcare system. Aisha and her team compiled these stories, creating a powerful narrative of healthcare inequality that became the backbone of their campaign.

"This is about life and death," Aisha said at one of their rallies. "Our communities are being denied the care they need, and we're not going to stand for it any longer."

Chapter 59: A Broken System

The healthcare system, like so many others they had fought against, was controlled by powerful forces—insurance companies, pharmaceutical corporations, and hospital executives. These industries were driven by profit, not by the well-being of the people, and they had deep pockets and political connections.

Aisha and her team quickly realized that this battle would be different from the others. They were no longer just fighting against local politicians or developers; they were taking on a system that was national in scope, one that had long resisted reform.

"Healthcare is a business," Danielle said during a strategy meeting. "The people who run it aren't going to give up their profits without a fight."

But Aisha knew they couldn't back down. The stakes were too high. They began working with healthcare advocates, nurses' unions, and community health organizations to develop a comprehensive plan for healthcare reform. Their demands included expanding access to healthcare in underserved neighborhoods, increasing funding for community clinics, and implementing stronger protections for patients.

The team also began lobbying local and state governments to support initiatives that would address the healthcare crisis. They knew that tackling such a deeply entrenched system would require both grassroots activism and policy change.

Chapter 60: Health as a Human Right

As the campaign gained momentum, Aisha and her team framed healthcare as a human rights issue. They organized marches and rallies under the banner "Health is a Human Right," demanding that the government prioritize healthcare for all people, not just those who could afford it.

At one of the rallies, Aisha stood in front of a large crowd, her voice ringing with conviction. "Healthcare is not a privilege for the wealthy. It is a right. No one should be denied care because of the size of their paycheck. We are demanding that the government and the healthcare system treat us with the dignity and respect we deserve."

The movement quickly gained traction. Healthcare workers, doctors, and nurses began to join the protests, adding their voices to the call for reform. Many of them had witnessed firsthand the consequences of an unequal system, and they were tired of seeing their patients suffer.

Dr. Patel, a physician who worked in one of the city's underfunded hospitals, spoke at one of the rallies. "I see it every day," she said. "Patients who come in too late because they couldn't afford care. Children who go untreated because their parents can't afford their medications. This is not healthcare—it's a failure of our society to protect its most vulnerable."

Aisha knew that they had tapped into something powerful. The issue of healthcare affected everyone, and the movement was gaining momentum as more people realized that the system was failing them.

Chapter 61: Fighting the Corporate Machine

As the movement grew, so did the opposition. The healthcare industry, feeling threatened by the growing calls for reform, launched a massive public relations campaign to discredit the movement. Ads flooded the airwaves, warning that the reforms Aisha and her team were calling for would lead to "socialized medicine" and "government overreach."

The insurance companies and pharmaceutical corporations were relentless, spending millions to sway public opinion. They used scare tactics, claiming that expanding healthcare access would lead to longer wait times, higher taxes, and lower-quality care.

But Aisha wasn't deterred. She had faced powerful opponents before, and she knew that their tactics were designed to sow fear and confusion.

"They're afraid," Aisha said during a meeting with her core team. "They're afraid because they know we're right. They know that people are waking up to the fact that the system is rigged, and they're doing everything they can to hold onto their profits. But we're not going to let them."

The team responded by launching their own public education campaign, using social media, community meetings, and public forums to counter the misinformation being spread by the healthcare industry. They worked with doctors and healthcare experts to explain how the reforms would benefit the public and improve the quality of care.

"We're not asking for handouts," Aisha said during one of their televised interviews. "We're asking for a system that works for everyone, not just the wealthy. We're asking for a system that puts people before profits."

Chapter 62: The People's Health Plan

After months of organizing, the movement unveiled "The People's Health Plan," a comprehensive set of reforms aimed at transforming the city's healthcare system. The plan called for increased funding for public hospitals and clinics, protections for patients against predatory insurance practices, and the creation of a public healthcare option that would provide affordable coverage to all residents.

The plan was ambitious, and it sparked intense debate in the city council. Some council members, backed by the healthcare industry, argued that the plan was too expensive and would bankrupt the city. But Aisha and her team had done their homework, and they had the numbers to back up their proposals.

"This isn't just about dollars and cents," Aisha said during a city council hearing. "This is about people's lives. We can't afford not to act."

The council chambers were packed with supporters, many of whom held signs that read "Healthcare for All" and "People Over Profits." The public pressure was immense, and Aisha knew that the council members were feeling it.

The vote on The People's Health Plan was scheduled for the following month, and in the meantime, Aisha and her team worked tirelessly to build support. They organized marches, held town halls, and met with key decision-makers to ensure that the plan would pass.

Chapter 63: A Step Toward Justice

The day of the vote arrived, and the city was on edge. The healthcare industry had spent millions trying to defeat The People's Health Plan, but Aisha and her team had mobilized a groundswell of support. The council chambers were filled with healthcare workers, patients, activists, and community members, all waiting to see if the city would take a stand for healthcare justice.

When the final vote came in, the plan passed by a narrow margin. The room erupted in cheers, and Aisha felt a wave of relief and triumph. They had done it. They had won.

Later that night, as Aisha and her team celebrated the victory, she reflected on how far they had come. The healthcare fight had been one of the toughest battles they had faced, but they had proven once again that when people came together, they could win—even against the most powerful forces.

"We've taken a huge step today," Aisha said as she addressed the crowd of supporters. "But this is just the beginning. Healthcare is a human right, and we're going to keep fighting until every person in this city, and in this country, has access to the care they need."

Chapter 64: The Politics of Power

As the movement continued to secure victories in healthcare, housing, education, and police reform, Aisha found herself in uncharted territory. The movement was no longer just a grassroots organization fighting for justice on the streets—it had become a political force, shaping policies and influencing decisions in city hall and beyond. With that influence came new challenges and responsibilities, ones that Aisha hadn't fully anticipated.

City leaders, politicians, and even national figures were taking notice of Aisha and her team's growing influence. Offers for partnerships, endorsements, and speaking engagements poured in. Some politicians wanted to align themselves with the movement, hoping to ride the wave of popular support that Aisha had built. Others saw the movement's success as a threat and began quietly working to undermine it.

"The more power we gain, the more enemies we make," Jason said one evening as they discussed their next steps. "They're not going to let us keep winning without a fight."

Aisha knew he was right. The victories they had won were not just about policies—they were about shifting the balance of power in the city. And with each victory, the opposition grew more determined to stop them. But Aisha was not deterred. She had always known that the fight for justice was about power—who had it, who didn't, and how to change that dynamic.

"We can't be afraid of power," Aisha said, her voice firm. "We've earned this influence, and we're going to use it. But we have to be smart. We can't let them turn us into something we're not."

The challenge now was to navigate the political landscape without losing sight of the movement's original vision. Aisha knew that staying true to their principles while wielding power was a delicate balance, but it was one she was determined to maintain.

Chapter 65: Power and Principle

As the movement's influence grew, so did the pressure to compromise. Political leaders and corporate interests who had once dismissed the movement were now approaching Aisha with offers of partnership and collaboration. Some of these offers came with promises of funding and resources—things the movement desperately needed to sustain its work. But they also came with strings attached.

Danielle, always the strategist, had been fielding calls from potential allies and donors for weeks. "They're dangling big money in front of us," she said during a strategy meeting. "But they want something in return. They want to shape our message, soften our demands, and turn us into something more palatable to their interests."

Aisha shook her head, her expression hardening. "That's not who we are. We didn't get this far by playing nice with the people who caused these problems in the first place. If we start compromising now, we lose everything we've fought for."

But it wasn't just about money. As the movement's political influence grew, some within the coalition began pushing for Aisha to run for office. They argued that her leadership and vision could make a bigger impact from within the system, where she could push for even more sweeping reforms.

"You should think about it," Jason said one evening after a long day of meetings. "You've got the support, and you've proven that you can lead. If you ran for office, you could change the system from the inside."

Aisha was torn. She had always believed in the power of grassroots organizing and had built the movement outside the political system. Running for office seemed like a departure from that, but she also knew that real change often required working from within.

"I don't know if that's the right move," Aisha said, her voice heavy with uncertainty. "I've spent my whole life fighting against the system. I'm not sure I can be part of it."

But the idea lingered in her mind, and as the pressure mounted, Aisha found herself grappling with the question of how to wield the power she had gained without losing her identity or the movement's core values.

Chapter 66: The Cost of Compromise

As Aisha and her team navigated their growing political influence, they began to feel the strain of internal divisions. The movement had always been made up of a diverse coalition of activists, community leaders, and organizations, each with their own priorities and visions for change. Now, as the movement became more powerful, those differences were becoming harder to reconcile.

Some members of the coalition, particularly the younger activists like Marcus, were growing frustrated with what they saw as the movement's increasing willingness to compromise. They believed that Aisha and her team were losing sight of the movement's radical roots, and that by working with politicians and corporate interests, they were diluting their message.

"We didn't start this movement to play by their rules," Marcus said during a heated meeting. "We started this to tear the system down, not to make deals with the people who are part of the problem."

Aisha listened, understanding his frustration but also knowing that their growing power required a different approach. "I get it," she said, her voice calm but firm. "But if we want to make real change, we have to be strategic. We can't tear the system down overnight, and we can't do it alone. We need allies, and we need resources."

Marcus wasn't convinced. "But at what cost? How much are we willing to give up just to win a few battles? We're losing who we are."

The tension in the room was palpable, and Aisha knew that this was a pivotal moment for the movement. They had to find a way to balance their radical vision with the realities of political power, or risk fracturing the coalition they had worked so hard to build.

Chapter 67: The Fight for the Future

As the movement grappled with its internal divisions, Aisha began to think more deeply about the future—both for herself and for the movement. The question of whether to run for office loomed large in her mind, and she found herself seeking advice from trusted allies and mentors.

One evening, Aisha sat down with Denise, the labor union leader who had been one of her earliest supporters. Denise had seen the movement grow from a small group of activists into a political force, and she understood the challenges Aisha was facing.

"You've got a big decision to make," Denise said, her voice steady. "Running for office would give you a platform to push for even bigger changes, but it also comes with a lot of baggage. Politics is a dirty game, and once you're in it, you're playing by their rules."

Aisha nodded, her thoughts swirling. "That's what I'm afraid of. I don't want to become part of the system we've been fighting against."

Denise smiled gently. "But here's the thing—you've already changed the system. You've already shown them that they can't ignore us anymore. Whether you run for office or not, you're already a force to be reckoned with. The question is, how do you want to use that power?"

Aisha thought about Denise's words long after their conversation ended. She knew that whatever decision she made, it would shape the future of the movement and her role within it.

Chapter 68: A New Direction

After weeks of reflection and discussions with her team, Aisha made her decision: she would not run for office. While the idea of holding political power was tempting, Aisha knew that her strength—and the strength of the movement—lay in its independence from the system. They had built their power from the ground up, and Aisha was determined to keep it that way.

At a press conference, Aisha announced her decision, making it clear that the movement's work was far from over. "We've made incredible progress, but we're not done yet. We've shown that we can change the system from the outside, and that's where our power lies. We don't need to play by their rules to win. We've built something that will last, and we're going to keep pushing for justice—on our terms."

The announcement was met with mixed reactions. Some were disappointed that Aisha had chosen not to run, believing that she could have achieved even more from within the system. But many, especially the grassroots activists who had been with her from the beginning, were relieved.

"We're stronger because we're independent," Jason said after the press conference. "We've got the freedom to fight on our own terms, and that's what makes us dangerous to them."

Aisha felt a sense of clarity and purpose. The movement didn't need to be absorbed into the political machine to make a difference. They were already making history, and they were going to keep doing it their way.

Chapter 69: A Movement Renewed

With the decision behind her, Aisha threw herself back into the work of the movement. They continued to push for reforms in healthcare, housing, education, and criminal justice, but they also began to expand their focus to new issues, such as environmental justice and workers' rights. The movement was evolving, and Aisha was determined to keep it growing.

One of the most important steps they took was to invest in leadership development, training a new generation of activists to carry the movement forward. Aisha knew that the future of the movement didn't rest solely on her shoulders—it was a collective effort, and the more leaders they could cultivate, the stronger they would be.

"We're building something that's going to outlast all of us," Aisha said during a leadership retreat. "This movement isn't about any one person—it's about all of us, working together to create the future we want. And we're going to keep fighting, no matter what."

The movement was stronger than ever, and Aisha felt a renewed sense of purpose. They had faced immense challenges, and there were more battles ahead, but they had built something that was resilient, something that could withstand the pressures of power and politics.

Chapter 70: The Long Game

As Aisha and her team looked to the future, they knew that the fight for justice was a long one. They had won major victories, but the systems they were fighting against were deeply entrenched, and real change would take time.

But Aisha was no longer daunted by the long road ahead. She had learned that the fight for justice wasn't about quick wins or easy victories—it was about persistence, resilience, and a commitment to the people they were fighting for.

"We're playing the long game," Aisha said during a meeting with her core team. "And we're in this for the long haul. We've built something that's going to last, and we're going to keep pushing until we've created the world we know is possible."

The movement had grown from a small group of activists into a powerful force for change, and Aisha knew that their work was far from over. But she also knew that they were ready for whatever came next.

Together, they had changed the city—and they were just getting started.

Chapter 71: A New Coalition

With their victories stacking up and the movement gaining both local and national attention, Aisha and her team saw an opportunity to expand their reach even further. While their work had transformed the city in significant ways, they realized that many of the issues they were fighting—healthcare inequality, environmental degradation, housing injustice—were not confined to their city. These were national and even global issues. It was time to broaden their scope and build a coalition that could take on these challenges on a larger scale.

Aisha had always believed that their movement was part of something bigger. Now, it was time to make that belief a reality.

"We've changed this city," Aisha said during a meeting with her core team, "but we can't stop here. The same systems we've fought against are hurting people all over this country. If we want real, lasting change, we need to build alliances, form coalitions, and connect with movements in other cities and states. It's time to think bigger."

Jason, who had been in contact with activists across the country, agreed. "There are groups out there fighting the same fights—environmental justice, workers' rights, healthcare access. If we join forces, we'll be unstoppable. We can take what we've done here and multiply it across the country."

Aisha knew that forming a coalition wasn't just about growing their power; it was about solidarity. The issues they were fighting were deeply interconnected, and they couldn't solve them in isolation. By building alliances with other movements, they could create a united front that had the power to demand change on a national level.

Chapter 72: Building Bridges

The first step in forming the coalition was reaching out to national organizations and movements that shared their values and goals. Aisha and her team began by connecting with environmental justice groups, workers' rights organizations, and healthcare advocates. They attended conferences, held joint meetings, and started to build relationships with leaders from across the country.

One of the most important connections they made was with an environmental justice group that had been fighting against toxic waste dumps in low-income neighborhoods. The group, led by a charismatic young activist named Malikah, had been making waves in the national media for its bold protests and legal battles against powerful corporations.

"We've been watching your work," Malikah said during their first meeting. "You've done something incredible in your city, and we want to work with you to take this fight to the next level."

Aisha felt an immediate connection with Malikah, who shared her passion for justice and her determination to take on the powerful forces that were harming their communities. Together, they began to strategize about how to link their movements and create a national coalition that could address both environmental and social justice issues.

"We're fighting the same fight," Malikah said. "Whether it's toxic waste, healthcare inequality, or police brutality, it's all connected. The same systems that are poisoning our air and water are the ones denying people healthcare and housing. We need to attack this from all sides."

Aisha couldn't have agreed more. The coalition was starting to take shape, and with it, the potential for real, systemic change on a national scale.

Chapter 73: Uniting for Justice

As the coalition grew, Aisha and her team began organizing a series of national forums and summits, bringing together activists, community leaders, and policymakers from across the country. The goal was to create a unified platform that addressed the interconnected issues of economic justice, environmental sustainability, healthcare access, and civil rights.

The first summit, held in their city, drew hundreds of activists and organizers from all over the country. It was a powerful moment, a symbol of the growing movement for justice that was sweeping the nation.

"We're here because we believe in a better future," Aisha said as she addressed the crowd. "A future where everyone has access to healthcare, housing, clean air, and water. A future where justice isn't just a word—it's a reality for everyone. This coalition is about building that future together."

The response was overwhelming. Activists from all corners of the country shared their stories, their struggles, and their victories. They strategized, exchanged ideas, and committed to working together to tackle the systemic issues that were affecting their communities.

By the end of the summit, the coalition had a clear vision: they would fight for justice on all fronts, using their collective power to demand systemic change at the local, state, and national levels. It was an ambitious vision, but Aisha knew that with the right alliances, it was possible.

Chapter 74: New Frontiers

With the coalition in place, Aisha and her team began working on a series of national campaigns. They focused on issues that crossed city and state lines: environmental racism, corporate greed, labor rights, and healthcare access. These campaigns were designed to put pressure on both local governments and federal policymakers to address the deep-rooted inequalities that were harming marginalized communities.

One of the most pressing issues they tackled was climate justice. The coalition launched a campaign to stop the construction of a massive oil pipeline that would run through several low-income and Indigenous communities, threatening their land and water. Aisha and her team partnered with environmental groups, Indigenous activists, and legal advocates to stop the pipeline in its tracks.

"This isn't just about stopping a pipeline," Aisha said during a press conference. "This is about protecting our communities from environmental destruction and corporate greed. We're fighting for the right to clean air, clean water, and a future that isn't destroyed by short-term profits."

The fight against the pipeline became a rallying cry for the coalition, and it drew national attention. Protests erupted across the country, with thousands of people joining the movement to demand environmental justice.

Chapter 75: Challenges of Scale

As the coalition grew and its influence spread, Aisha began to feel the weight of leading such a vast and complex movement. The issues they were tackling—environmental justice, labor rights, healthcare access—were interconnected but also required different strategies and expertise. Coordinating efforts across multiple states and organizations was a monumental task, and it stretched the resources of Aisha's team to the limit.

"There are so many moving parts," Jason said one evening as they reviewed their plans. "We're fighting battles on so many fronts, and it's hard to keep everyone on the same page."

Aisha nodded, feeling the strain herself. The coalition was powerful, but it also required constant communication, coordination, and decision-making. She had to balance the needs of local campaigns with the broader goals of the national movement, all while keeping the momentum going.

"We need to build more leadership," Aisha said. "We can't do this alone. We need to train more people to take on leadership roles in the coalition, so we're not spread so thin."

The team began developing a leadership training program for activists across the country, empowering them to take on more responsibility within the coalition. It was a necessary step to ensure that the movement could grow without losing its focus or energy.

Chapter 76: A Global Perspective

As the coalition expanded, Aisha and her team began to see that the issues they were fighting were not just national—they were global. Environmental degradation, labor exploitation, and healthcare inequality were problems faced by marginalized communities around the world. The same corporations that polluted their city were operating in other countries, exploiting natural resources and harming vulnerable populations.

Aisha realized that if they wanted to truly address these issues, they needed to think globally. She began reaching out to international organizations and activists, forging connections with movements in Latin America, Africa, and Asia. These alliances added a new dimension to the coalition's work, creating opportunities for collaboration on a global scale.

One of the most powerful moments came when Aisha was invited to speak at an international climate justice summit in Brazil. There, she met activists from all over the world who were fighting similar battles against environmental destruction and corporate greed.

"This is a global fight," Aisha said during her speech at the summit. "The forces we're up against don't respect borders—they exploit communities everywhere. But just as they are global, so are we. We are building a movement that crosses borders, that unites people from all walks of life, and that fights for a future where justice and sustainability are not just dreams, but realities."

Chapter 77: The Strength of Solidarity

Back at home, the coalition continued to grow in strength and influence. They launched new campaigns focused on economic justice, demanding higher wages, better working conditions, and protections for workers in industries like agriculture, healthcare, and retail. They partnered with unions, workers' rights groups, and community organizations to organize strikes and protests, putting pressure on corporations and policymakers to address the exploitation of workers.

The coalition's power lay in its ability to bring together people from all walks of life—workers, environmentalists, healthcare advocates, civil rights activists—around a shared vision of justice. It wasn't always easy to keep everyone united, but Aisha knew that their strength lay in their solidarity.

"We are stronger together," Aisha said during one of their rallies. "We may come from different places, we may fight on different fronts, but we are united by our belief in justice. And as long as we stand together, there is nothing we can't achieve."

Chapter 78: Facing the Backlash

As the coalition gained more victories and its influence spread, the backlash from corporate interests, conservative politicians, and powerful elites grew stronger. The opposition launched a massive campaign to discredit the movement, framing them as radical, out-of-touch extremists who wanted to upend the economy and destroy jobs.

The media, funded by corporate interests, ran smear campaigns against Aisha and her team, portraying them as dangerous agitators. Conservative politicians introduced legislation to curb the influence of activist groups, and law enforcement agencies began to crack down on protests with increasing aggression.

"They're scared," Jason said one night after another round of negative media coverage. "They're pulling out all the stops to try to stop us."

Aisha knew that the backlash was a sign that they were making an impact, but it was also exhausting. The constant attacks, both personal and political, took a toll on her and the team. But she refused to back down.

"They can smear us all they want," Aisha said. "But we're not going anywhere. We're going to keep fighting, and we're going to keep winning."

Chapter 79: A Movement Under Fire

As the coalition's influence grew, so did the intensity of the opposition's efforts to undermine it. Corporate interests and conservative political leaders were no longer content with smear campaigns and negative media coverage—they began pushing for legislative and legal measures to weaken the movement. Across the country, states introduced laws designed to curb protests, increase penalties for civil disobedience, and restrict the activities of activist organizations. It was clear that the coalition's success was seen as a direct threat to the status quo, and powerful forces were mobilizing to stop them.

The crackdowns started slowly. Protesters were met with increasing aggression from law enforcement, with peaceful demonstrations being dispersed by riot police, tear gas, and mass arrests. Organizers were targeted with legal threats, and some coalition members even faced charges designed to intimidate them into silence.

Aisha, who had been the face of the movement for so long, found herself under constant surveillance. There were attempts to frame her and other key leaders as extremists, and threats against her personal safety increased.

"They're scared because we're winning," Jason said during one of their many strategy meetings as they discussed the rising wave of repression. "They want to break us before we gain any more ground."

Aisha nodded, her expression serious but determined. "We can't let them intimidate us. This is what happens when you challenge power—they try to silence you. But we're not going to be silenced."

The movement had faced opposition before, but this was a new level of repression. Aisha and her team knew they had to be strategic in how they moved forward. They had to protect their members, keep the momentum going, and find new ways to fight back against a system that was trying to crush them.

Chapter 80: Legal Battles and Resistance

One of the coalition's primary concerns was the wave of anti-protest laws being passed across the country. These laws, often backed by corporate interests and conservative politicians, sought to criminalize dissent by imposing severe penalties on protesters and organizers. The laws were designed to weaken the coalition by making it riskier for people to take to the streets and by draining the movement's resources through legal battles.

Aisha and her team worked closely with civil rights lawyers to challenge these laws in court. They launched a series of lawsuits, arguing that the laws were unconstitutional and violated the rights of free speech and assembly. The legal battles were long and grueling, but they were necessary to protect the coalition's ability to organize and protest.

"We can't let them legislate us out of existence," Aisha said during a meeting with their legal team. "This is about more than just one protest—it's about our right to be heard."

The legal battles were fought on multiple fronts, with some cases making it all the way to the federal courts. It was a slow, exhausting process, but Aisha knew that they had to keep pushing. The courts were one battleground, but the streets were another.

Even as the legal battles raged on, the coalition continued to organize protests, marches, and strikes. They knew that if they backed down, the opposition would see it as a victory. Instead, they doubled down, launching a series of high-profile actions that kept the public's attention on their demands for justice.

Chapter 81: State Surveillance and Harassment

The repression went beyond legal challenges. Aisha and other key leaders in the coalition became the targets of state surveillance and harassment. Their phones were tapped, their emails monitored, and their movements tracked. At protests, organizers reported being followed by unmarked cars, and some coalition members received anonymous threats meant to intimidate them into silence.

It was clear that the state was using its power to try to weaken the movement from within, sowing fear and distrust among its members.

"We're under a microscope," Danielle said one evening as they discussed the escalating surveillance. "They're trying to scare us into making mistakes, into turning on each other."

Aisha knew that fear was one of the most powerful weapons used against movements. If they let it seep into their ranks, it could fracture the coalition and undo all the work they had accomplished. But she also knew that they had to be cautious. The stakes were higher than ever, and the consequences of a misstep could be devastating.

"We need to stay focused," Aisha said. "We know what they're trying to do, and we can't let it work. We're going to protect each other, and we're going to keep fighting."

The team began taking precautions. They encrypted their communications, used secure channels for organizing, and implemented security protocols for their leadership. It was a new way of working, one that was necessary in the face of increasing repression.

But even as they adapted, Aisha felt the weight of the surveillance pressing down on her. She had always known that fighting for justice meant making sacrifices, but now those sacrifices felt more personal than ever.

Chapter 82: Keeping the Fire Burning

Despite the escalating repression, the coalition refused to back down. If anything, the crackdowns fueled their resolve. The more the state and corporate interests tried to silence them, the more determined they became to keep pushing for justice.

"We've been here before," Jason said during one particularly difficult week when several coalition members had been arrested during a protest. "This isn't new. They've always tried to silence movements, but they've never succeeded."

Aisha agreed. She had studied the history of civil rights movements, labor movements, and environmental movements. Repression was part of the process, but so was resistance. The coalition had been built on the foundation of resilience, and Aisha knew that if they stood together, they could withstand whatever was thrown at them.

The coalition began organizing teach-ins and workshops to educate new members on the history of repression and how to resist it. They taught people how to stay safe during protests, how to handle encounters with law enforcement, and how to protect their rights. It wasn't just about organizing—it was about building a culture of resilience.

"We're not just fighting for justice," Aisha said during one of the teach-ins. "We're fighting to protect each other, to build a community that can stand strong even in the face of repression. This is about survival, and we're going to survive."

Chapter 83: Strength in Numbers

One of the most powerful strategies the coalition employed during this period of repression was expanding their base of support. They knew that the more people they had on their side, the harder it would be for the state to crush them. They reached out to unions, community organizations, churches, and student groups, building alliances that made the coalition stronger.

Aisha and her team organized a National Day of Action, bringing together thousands of people from across the country to protest the wave of anti-protest laws and state repression. The day of action was a powerful show of solidarity, with rallies held in dozens of cities and thousands of people taking to the streets.

"We're sending a message," Aisha said at the rally in their city. "We will not be silenced. We will not be intimidated. We are many, and we are strong. This is just the beginning."

The National Day of Action was a success, drawing widespread media attention and putting pressure on lawmakers to reconsider repressive laws. It also demonstrated the power of the coalition—by standing together, they were able to amplify their voices and demand change on a larger scale.

Chapter 84: The Tipping Point

The coalition's relentless organizing, combined with their legal battles and public pressure, began to pay off. In several states, courts struck down the most draconian anti-protest laws, ruling that they violated constitutional rights. At the same time, public opinion was beginning to shift. The more the state and corporate interests tried to silence the movement, the more people began to see through the tactics of repression.

Aisha and her team knew that they had reached a tipping point. The opposition was still powerful, but the coalition had proven that it could withstand the attacks. They had built a movement that was resilient, adaptable, and capable of surviving even the most intense repression.

But Aisha also knew that the fight wasn't over. The forces they were up against would continue to push back, and the road ahead was still long. But for the first time in months, she felt a sense of hope.

"We've been through hell," Aisha said during a meeting with her core team. "But we're still here. And we're not just surviving—we're winning. We've proven that we can stand up to them, and now we're going to keep pushing until we've won the justice we deserve."

Chapter 85: A Vision for the Future

With the coalition stronger than ever, Aisha and her team began to look toward the future. They had weathered the storm of repression, but they knew that their fight was far from over. The issues they were tackling—healthcare, environmental justice, labor rights, and civil rights—were deeply entrenched, and real change would take time.

But Aisha also knew that they had built something powerful. They had created a movement that wasn't just about protest—it was about building a new vision for the future. A future where justice wasn't just a slogan but a reality for everyone.

As they gathered for a leadership retreat to plan their next steps, Aisha felt a deep sense of pride in what they had accomplished. They had taken on some of the most powerful forces in the country and emerged stronger for it.

"This movement isn't just about resistance," Aisha said as she addressed the leaders of the coalition. "It's about creation. We're not just fighting against something—we're building something new. And together, we're going to create a future where justice, equality, and dignity are the foundation of our society."

The road ahead would still be difficult, but Aisha knew that they were ready. They had survived the repression, built a powerful coalition, and inspired a new generation of activists. The fight for justice would continue, and Aisha was ready to lead the way.

Chapter 86: Creating a New World

With the coalition stronger than ever and having survived the worst of the state repression, Aisha and her team began to focus on a new goal: building alternative systems of care, sustainability, and justice. While their battles for healthcare, environmental justice, and labor rights had secured major victories, Aisha knew that lasting change required more than just reforming existing systems. It meant creating new structures that reflected their vision of a just, equitable society.

For Aisha, this next phase was about building a model for the future. The coalition had proven that they could challenge the status quo, but now they wanted to show what was possible beyond resistance—how communities could thrive outside the constraints of corporate control, systemic inequality, and environmental destruction.

"We've been fighting to change the system," Aisha said during one of their planning meetings. "But what if we built something better? What if we didn't just fight for healthcare, education, and justice—we created our own systems that work for us, right now?"

The idea was ambitious, but Aisha knew that they had the power to bring it to life. The coalition was filled with visionaries, organizers, and community leaders who were ready to take the next step. Together, they could begin to create the future they had always fought for.

Chapter 87: Building Community Care

The first step was to create systems of community care. Healthcare had always been a core issue for the coalition, but many people in marginalized communities still struggled to access affordable, quality care. Aisha and her team began working with doctors, nurses, and healthcare professionals within the movement to set up community health clinics that provided free or low-cost services.

These clinics didn't just focus on treating illness—they focused on holistic care. They offered mental health services, nutritional counseling, and preventive care, all with a focus on addressing the root causes of health disparities in marginalized communities.

Dr. Patel, a longtime supporter of the movement, took the lead on organizing the clinics. "This is what healthcare should look like," she said as she walked Aisha through the newly opened clinic. "Care that's accessible, compassionate, and rooted in the community. We're not just treating symptoms here—we're treating people, and we're giving them the tools they need to thrive."

The clinics became a symbol of what the coalition was working toward: a world where communities took care of each other, where people had access to the resources, they needed without having to navigate bureaucratic systems that often denied them care.

Chapter 88: Sustainable Living and Environmental Justice

As the coalition expanded its vision, they also began focusing on environmental sustainability. For years, they had fought against environmental racism and the destruction caused by corporate greed, but now they wanted to create solutions that would protect the planet and ensure that communities had access to clean air, water, and healthy food.

Aisha partnered with Malikah and other environmental justice leaders to launch a series of community sustainability projects. They started by creating urban gardens and farming co-ops in areas that had long been food deserts. These gardens provided fresh produce to the community, gave people the opportunity to grow their own food, and created green spaces in neighborhoods that had been neglected for years.

"We're taking back our land," Malikah said as they planted the first garden in a vacant lot that had once been an industrial dumping ground. "We're not just healing the earth—we're healing our communities. This is how we build a sustainable future."

In addition to the gardens, the coalition worked on renewable energy projects, installing solar panels on community centers and schools, and promoting energy independence. They partnered with engineers and environmentalists to create solutions that were accessible to everyone, not just the wealthy.

These projects were a tangible expression of the coalition's values—an acknowledgment that environmental justice was inseparable from social justice, and that true freedom meant being able to live in harmony with the earth.

Chapter 89: Education for Liberation

Education had always been a cornerstone of the movement, but Aisha and her team wanted to take it a step further. Beyond fighting for funding and reforms within the public school system, they wanted to create alternative educational spaces that empowered young people to think critically, understand their history, and imagine new possibilities for the future.

The coalition began working with teachers, activists, and scholars to create "liberation schools," where students could learn about social justice, environmental sustainability, and community organizing. These schools focused on teaching students how to be leaders in their communities, how to fight for change, and how to build a future rooted in justice and equality.

"These aren't just schools," said Maya, who had become one of the leading voices in the education movement. "These are spaces where young people can learn to dream, to imagine, and to create the world they want to live in. We're teaching them that they have the power to change the world."

The liberation schools were designed to be free and accessible to all, with a curriculum that was created by and for the community. They offered classes in history, economics, environmental science, and social justice, but they also provided opportunities for students to engage in hands-on projects, like building community gardens, organizing protests, and creating art that reflected their vision of the future.

For Aisha, the liberation schools represented a new chapter in the movement. They weren't just fighting for change—they were preparing the next generation to lead it.

Chapter 90: Justice Through Economic Cooperation

Economic justice had always been a central part of the coalition's work, but now they were thinking beyond traditional labor organizing and minimum wage fights. Aisha and her team wanted to create alternative economic systems that were rooted in cooperation, not exploitation.

They began by setting up worker-owned cooperatives, where employees had a say in how their businesses were run and shared in the profits. These co-ops provided jobs, empowered workers, and created a model for how the economy could work for everyone, not just the wealthy.

Denise, the labor leader who had been with the movement from the beginning, took charge of organizing the co-ops. "This is what real economic justice looks like," she said as she led a meeting of workers who were launching a cooperative bakery. "We're not just fighting for higher wages—we're creating businesses that are owned by the people, for the people. This is how we take control of our economic future."

The worker co-ops became an essential part of the coalition's vision for the future. They showed that it was possible to create an economy that valued people over profits, where workers had control over their livelihoods and where wealth was shared more equitably.

Chapter 91: The Power of Art and Culture

Art had always been a powerful tool for the movement, but Aisha knew that it could play an even bigger role in shaping their vision for the future. Art had the power to inspire, to challenge, and to imagine new worlds, and Aisha wanted to harness that power to build a culture of resistance and resilience.

The coalition partnered with artists, musicians, writers, and filmmakers to create cultural projects that reflected their vision of justice. They organized art festivals, music concerts, and film screenings that celebrated the struggles and triumphs of marginalized communities.

"We're creating a new culture," said Danielle, who had taken the lead on organizing the coalition's cultural initiatives. "A culture that reflects who we are, that tells our stories, and that inspires people to fight for justice. Art is more than just a reflection of the world—it's a way to shape the future."

The coalition's cultural projects became a key part of their organizing strategy, drawing people into the movement and creating spaces where they could express their hopes, fears, and dreams. Through art, Aisha and her team were able to reach people who had never been involved in activism before, inspiring them to join the fight for justice.

Chapter 92: A New Model for Society

As the coalition's projects took shape, Aisha began to see that they were building more than just a movement—they were building a model for a new society. The clinics, gardens, schools, co-ops, and cultural initiatives were all part of a larger vision: a world where people took care of each other, where communities were empowered, and where justice and sustainability were at the center of everything.

"We're not just resisting anymore," Aisha said during a gathering of coalition leaders. "We're creating. We're showing the world what's possible when we put people first, when we reject the systems that have harmed us, and when we build something new. This is what the future looks like."

The coalition's work began to attract attention from other cities and countries. People came from all over to learn about the clinics, the co-ops, the liberation schools, and the sustainability projects. They wanted to know how they could bring these models back to their own communities, how they could replicate the coalition's success.

For Aisha, this was the ultimate victory. They had not only fought for justice—they had built it. They had created a new world, and that world was growing.

Chapter 93: Scaling the Vision

As the coalition's alternative systems of care, sustainability, and justice flourished, Aisha and her team began receiving invitations from other cities and movements eager to learn from their success. The clinics, worker-owned cooperatives, urban gardens, and liberation schools had become models for communities seeking to create change on their own terms. The question now was how to share that vision in a way that could be adapted to different contexts while maintaining the principles that had guided the coalition from the start.

Aisha understood that scaling their vision required more than just replicating their projects. It was about empowering other communities to take ownership of the ideas and make them their own. The beauty of what they had built was that it was rooted in the specific needs and desires of their community, and Aisha wanted to ensure that other movements could adapt those principles to fit their unique struggles.

"We're not here to tell people how to build their future," Aisha said during a meeting with coalition leaders. "We're here to share what we've learned, to offer support, and to inspire others to create something that works for them. This is about decentralizing power and giving it back to the people."

The team began organizing workshops and summits in cities across the country, inviting activists, community leaders, and organizers to learn about the coalition's model. They shared their successes, their challenges, and the lessons they had learned along the way, all with the goal of helping others create systems of justice and care in their own communities.

Chapter 94: Partnerships for Global Change

As the coalition's influence spread nationally, Aisha and her team also began to form partnerships with international movements. From climate activists in the Global South to labor organizers in Europe, the coalition was connecting with groups fighting for justice on a global scale. These movements, while different in many ways, shared the same goal: building a world where people and the planet came before profits.

One of the most significant partnerships was with an Indigenous-led movement in Central America that was fighting to protect their land from corporate exploitation. The two movements had much in common, particularly their commitment to environmental justice and community empowerment. Together, they began to explore ways to support each other's work, exchanging knowledge and resources in a spirit of solidarity.

"We're all fighting the same system," Malikah said during one of their planning meetings with international partners. "The corporations that exploit our land and labor don't care about borders, and neither should we. We need to stand together, across continents, to fight for our future."

This international collaboration allowed the coalition to see their work in a global context. The systems of injustice they had been fighting were not confined to their city or even their country—they were part of a global network of exploitation. By building alliances with movements across the world, they were taking the fight to a new level.

Chapter 95: Sharing the Blueprint

As the coalition grew in influence, Aisha and her team realized they needed a way to make their model more accessible to other movements. They decided to create a "blueprint for justice," a comprehensive guide that outlined the principles, strategies, and practices they had developed over the years. This blueprint wasn't a step-by-step manual—it was a living document that offered inspiration and guidance while encouraging communities to adapt the ideas to their own needs.

The blueprint included sections on healthcare, education, economic justice, environmental sustainability, and community organizing. It provided practical advice on how to set up worker-owned cooperatives, start community clinics, organize protests, and build liberation schools. But more importantly, it emphasized the importance of collective decision-making, local leadership, and grassroots empowerment.

"The blueprint is a tool," Aisha explained at the launch event. "It's a way to share what we've learned, but it's not the answer. Every community has its own needs, its own struggles, and its own solutions. This is about giving people the tools to build something that works for them."

The blueprint was made available online and in print, and it quickly spread across activist networks. Communities from around the world began using it to launch their own projects, adapting the principles to fit their local context. For Aisha and her team, this was the ultimate success: seeing their work inspire others to act and create change in their own ways.

Chapter 96: Facing New Challenges

As the coalition's model spread, new challenges emerged. With their growing influence came increased scrutiny from the very systems they were trying to dismantle. Corporations, conservative political leaders, and even some segments of the media launched new attacks against the coalition, accusing them of being "radicals" who were trying to disrupt the economy and society.

The opposition also became more sophisticated, co-opting some of the coalition's language and ideas to create watered-down versions of their initiatives. Corporations began promoting "green" projects that claimed to address environmental justice but were little more than PR stunts. Politicians introduced "progressive" policies that made symbolic gestures without addressing the root causes of inequality.

Aisha knew that these efforts were designed to undermine the coalition's work and divert public attention from the deeper systemic changes they were fighting for. But she also saw it as a sign that their ideas were having an impact.

"They wouldn't be trying to copy us if we weren't making a difference," Aisha said during a meeting with her core team. "But we need to be vigilant. We can't let them dilute what we're doing. We need to keep pushing for real, transformative change, not just surface-level fixes."

The team responded by doubling down on their commitment to grassroots organizing and community empowerment. They held forums and teach-ins to help people recognize the difference between genuine change and corporate greenwashing or political tokenism. They emphasized that their fight was not just about reform, it was about building a new world from the ground up.

Chapter 97: A New Generation Takes the Lead

As the coalition continued to grow, Aisha began to think more about the future. She had been at the forefront of the movement for years, but she knew that real, lasting change would require new leaders to take the helm. The liberation schools, worker cooperatives, and community clinics were all training grounds for the next generation of activists and organizers, and Aisha wanted to ensure that these new leaders had the tools they needed to carry the movement forward.

Maya, who had been a student activist and had grown into a key leader within the coalition, was one of the rising stars of this new generation. She was passionate, driven, and deeply committed to the movement's values of justice, equality, and sustainability. Aisha had mentored her for years, and she knew that Maya was ready to take on more responsibility.

At a leadership retreat, Aisha announced that she would be stepping back from her day-to-day role in the coalition to make space for new leaders to emerge. "This movement isn't about me," Aisha said, her voice filled with pride. "It's about all of us. It's about the future we're building together. And that future belongs to the next generation of leaders."

Maya and other young leaders stepped up, ready to carry the coalition forward. They brought fresh ideas, new energy, and a deep understanding of the struggles their generation was facing. Aisha knew that the movement was in good hands.

Chapter 98: The Global Movement for Justice

As the new generation of leaders took the reins of the coalition, the movement continued to grow on a global scale. The partnerships Aisha and her team had formed with international movements began to bear fruit, with joint campaigns and projects taking place across continents. From environmental justice in the Amazon to workers' rights in Southeast Asia, the coalition's influence was being felt far beyond their city.

Aisha, though no longer involved in the day-to-day operations, continued to play a role as an advisor and mentor to the global movement. She traveled to international conferences, met with world leaders, and helped build alliances that connected movements across borders.

"We're part of something bigger than any one country or city," Aisha said during a speech at a global summit. "This is a global fight for justice, for dignity, for the future of our planet. And together, we are unstoppable."

The global movement for justice was stronger than ever, and Aisha felt a deep sense of satisfaction in seeing the seeds she had planted grow into something so powerful and far-reaching.

Chapter 99: Reflections and Renewal

Years had passed since Aisha had first taken to the streets to protest police brutality and inequality. The coalition she had helped build had grown into a global movement for justice, and the world was beginning to change in ways she had only dreamed of. But as she reflected on her journey, Aisha knew that the work was never truly finished.

Sitting in her small office, surrounded by letters from activists around the world, Aisha took a moment to reflect on everything they had accomplished. They had built clinics, schools, cooperatives, and gardens. They had fought for healthcare, environmental justice, workers' rights, and civil rights. They had stood up to repression and state violence, and they had inspired countless others to do the same.

But Aisha also knew that the struggle for justice was ongoing. The systems they had been fighting were deeply entrenched, and new challenges would always arise. Yet, she felt hopeful. The movement was in good hands, and the new generation of leaders was ready to continue the fight.

"This is only the beginning," Aisha thought to herself. "The work we've started will live on, and the world we're building will only grow stronger."

Chapter 100: A World Reimagined

The movement had changed the world in ways that were once unimaginable. Communities across the globe had adopted the coalition's model, creating systems of care, justice, and sustainability that were transforming society from the ground up. Governments, corporations, and institutions were being forced to reckon with the power of people who had decided to take control of their own futures.

Aisha, now a global elder in the movement, looked out at the world she had helped shape. The fight for justice had been long and hard, but it had been worth every struggle, every sacrifice. The world was not perfect, but it was better. And the work continued.

"We've reimagined what's possible," Aisha said during a final public speech. "We've shown that justice isn't a dream—it's something we build, day by day, action by action, together. This is the world we've been fighting for. And it's only the beginning."

As Aisha stepped off the stage, she felt a sense of peace. The world she had helped create was in good hands, and the future was bright with possibility.

Don't miss out!

Visit the website below and you can sign up to receive emails whenever Selena Arnold publishes a new book. There's no charge and no obligation.

https://books2read.com/r/B-A-SZTDB-QBHDF

BOOKS 2 READ

Connecting independent readers to independent writers.

www.ingramcontent.com/pod-product-compliance
Lightning Source LLC
Chambersburg PA
CBHW061042250726
48653CB00001B/208